London 6-8-91

CYRIL FLETCHER'S GARDENING BOOK

ODD ODE

To write an ode on me I fear
Is not my usual cup of beer.
Indeed it isn't quite my scene
To write a book on fingers green.
I live far from the Metrollops—50 miles,
Where the lovely land of Sussex smiles
With glorious views of field and tree
And sunshine gleaming on the sea.
It inspired Turner to immortalise
The distant downs and sweeping skies.
And here to amuse my comic selve,
I sow and reap and mow and delve.
A TV Mogul knew of this,
Mingling horticulture and show buis.
And that is why from ATV
Gardening Today comes fortnightly,
And I appear with merry phiz
In answer to your gardening quiz.
I thought it might be so much better
Instead of answering every letter.
To say 'Dear Listener go and look,
You'll find it in my gardening book.'

CYRIL FLETCHER'S GARDENING BOOK

WILLIAM LUSCOMBE PUBLISHER LTD
(in association with Mitchell Beazley Ltd)

First published in Great Britain by
William Luscombe Publisher Ltd,
The Mitchell Beazley Group,
Artists House,
14–15 Manette Street,
London, W1V 5LB.
1974

ISBN 0 86002 013 4

Set and printed in Great Britain by
Butler & Tanner Ltd, Frome and London

Acknowledgements

I would like to acknowledge most gratefully the kind assistance I have received from: Beverley Nichols, for his kind help over lawns, and joyous gardening inspiration through the years; Nigel Nicolson for his kind permission to quote the wisdom of his mother, the late Vita Sackville-West, surely one of the greatest gardeners of all time, and Michael Joseph Ltd, the publishers of her *Garden Book*; Frederick (John) Street for valuable help received from his book *Rhododendrons* published by Cassells; Christopher Lloyd, who is almost a neighbour at Great Dixter, where he gardens with such expertise and shares his knowledge so charmingly with his writings on gardening, and especially his two books *Foliage Plants* and *The Well-Tempered Garden*, both published by Collins; Messrs Hilliers of Winchester, who have allowed me to use a little of the vast knowledge contained in their wonderful *Manual of Trees and Shrubs*, published by David & Charles; Mrs Desmond Underwood for knowledge garnered during my TV interview with her at the Royal Show; Isobel Barnett for letting me quote her *Woman's Hour* gardening hints; and finally Bob Price and Donald Shingler for their continuing inspiration.

That is one of the wonderful things about Gardeners. They are not only generous when giving you plants, etc., etc., but they are most generous, too, with their information.

CYRIL FLETCHER

Contents

Illustrations

Preface

I would like to dedicate this book to my dear friend Francis Essex who, as chief television executive, chose me to appear in the fortnightly ATV programme *Gardening Today*, thus almost turning my hobby into an auxiliary profession. Thank you, Francis, also, for the photograph of your well-head, a feature of your own lovely garden, which appears in the book.

I very much enjoy this programme which has now been running for over a year, and which so neatly joins my profession to my hobby. Once a fortnight I greatly look forward to meeting Bob Price—who adds his professional knowledge and expertise to my amateurism—and our producer Donald Shingler. Also our audience who write such charming letters and who send us, sometimes, very dead plants which arrive in an oleaginous mass with the query 'what do you think I should do with this?'

I would also like to thank my wife Betty for reading and amending grammatically this unlearned tome, and to her for sharing and inspiring the five gardens I have lovingly created for her through the happy years of our marriage.

Introduction

There is a murmur from the expectant audience. This is the magic moment when the footlights are switched on, illuminating the front-of-house curtains. The show is about to begin. 'Beginners, please!' has been shouted up the stairs or through the inter-com. The actors are standing in the wings, all ready for that moment when they walk on to the stage and confront the audience. The real beginners—that is to say the newcomers to the profession—will be nervous; the old hands will, as I do, feel not an attack of nerves, but a slight feeling of apprehension —it's really a desire to please and to do a good show. In my case it is a desire to get laughs. There is always an anxiety about this as every audience is different: different in IQ, different in mood, all differing in a thousand complexities. And oh, how when they are eager and receptive and ready to laugh, they get the best out of the performer, and how if they receive him coldly he may never recover from the first cold douche of their reception and then give his best. He will be battling and striving and worrying at the hard audience, but with the easy audience he will be as happy as they are, he will be relaxed and will, as it were, lean on their laughter and have time to give his performance a charm and a finesse which the hard audience would never get from him.

I wonder dear reader what kind of an audience are you? May I ask as Ruskin did 'Is your breath good and your temper!' It will need to be as I come falteringly out on to the stage, blinking into a strange new spotlight.

How can I begin? There was no better script-writer than William Shakespeare surely? What did he say? 'Come my spade. There is no ancient gentlemen but gardeners, ditchers and grave-makers; they hold up Adam's profession.'

We are setting out on an adventure. An exciting adventure. What could be more exciting than creating a work of art? And that is what we are about to do. We are going, Reader, you and I, to create a garden together. And no matter how small, how

13

modest, this garden will be a work of art. It may not be entirely successful, or indeed all that beautiful because, as with painters and sculptors and musicians, there will be degrees in our expertise. Some of us will be masters and some of us will be very modest 'trial by error' types as it were, Primitive painters. Also, the material we have to work with may be very inferior. We may have thick clay or salt-laden breezes, or sooty city fogs. We can be on top of a hill, deep in a frost hole, in the shade of great trees, or on arid sand; we may be trying to create a Versailles in a draughty corridor between two suburban houses. But wherever we are or whatever our advantages or disadvantages, a garden will result and because we have had fun doing it, and satisfaction out of our achievement, the result, no matter how unsuccessful, will be of a kind, a work of art. For a moment and very frequently (let's be honest) by accident we may create something exquisite—a minor work of art, but, and this is the delicious factor in gardening, we shall have to repeat it every year.

There is a something which makes our particular work of art even more satisfying than a picture, or sculpture, or a sonata. We are having to deal with the vagaries and vicissitudes of Mother Nature who can be a cruel mistress but, at the same time—and usually just when we don't expect it—kind and bountiful. Similarly, our site can curb our enthusiasms but then, sometimes, success can be achieved in spite of the apparent failure staring us in the face. I'll take a small example. You have a very damp shady corner. It's no good planting African marigolds, which need sun and well drained soil—you will never move the house next door which creates the shade, though you might, at great expense, drain your damp patch. No, the answer my friends, is to take advantage of your adversity. You make a garden of this damp patch and grow in it all those lovely flowers which love shade and damp—and grow them a damn sight better than your neighbour who has been trying for years to grow a hosta in full sun on sand!

So you see we are going to be crafty as well as artistic, and use to advantage every disadvantage, and also make the most of what we have. I am, of course, a comedian and not a professional gardener, but I am a very keen amateur and have been so for at least forty years. (No Madam, I began as a tiny child!) And because I am a keen amateur I have had all the amateur's heartbreaks and I have made all the amateur's mistakes. I am still learning and I hope in this book, as I share my many disasters and my few triumphs with you, I shall learn a little more.

POETIC LICENCE, I

Here damask-roses, white and red,
    Out of my lap first take I,
Which still shall run along the thread;
    My chiefest flower this make I.
Amongst these roses in a row,
    Next place I pinks in plenty,
These double daisies for a show,
    And will not this be dainty?
The pretty pansy then I'll tye
    Like stones some chain inchasing;
And next to them, their near ally
    The purple violet placing.
The curious choice clove July-flower,
    Whose kinds, hight the carnation,
For sweetness of most sovereign power
    Shall help my wreath to fashion;
Whose sundry colours of one kind,
    First from one root derivèd,
Them in their several suits I'll bind,
    My garland so contrivèd:
A course of cowslips then I'll stick,
    And here and there (though sparely)
The pleasant primrose down I'll prick,
    Like pearls which will show rarely:
Then with these marigolds I'll make
    My garland somewhat swelling,
These honeysuckles then I'll take,
    Whose sweets shall help their smelling.
The lily and the fleur-de-lis,
    For colour much contenting,
For that I them do only prize,
    They are but poor in scenting:
The daffodil most dainty is
    To match with these in meetness;
The columbine compared to this,
    All much alike for sweetness:

These in their natures only are
  Fit to emboss the border,
Therefore I'll take especial care
  To place them in their order:
Sweet-williams, campions, sops-in-wine,
  One by another neatly;
Thus have I made this wreath of mine,
  And finishèd it featly.

Michael Drayton (1563–1631)

1 Soil, Mulches and Compost

You are going to make a garden. You will have an entirely new bare patch or you will have an old garden which you are about to re-organise completely. Let us see what we have either to gloat over or to dismay us.

Size is immaterial. We can make a small garden seem large, or make it seem even smaller or more intimate. So we will not worry about size; it's usually something you can do little about anyway.

The soil is exceedingly important. If it is heavy clay we must lighten it. If it is sandy we must add humus to it. If it is chalky we must know our limitations on certain plants which will grow in it or not and, similarly, if it is acid we must know the degree of its acidity in case this needs amending. It is useful to know how deep the top-soil is; by that I mean have you a thin covering of soil under which there is solid rock—or perhaps quickly draining gravel? The ideal soil is an average loam which has preferably been worked. I once owned a water mill and the feel of the deep, dark, rich, alluvial soil which I had then fills moments of my happier dreams. The thick, heavy clay I'm encumbered with in my present garden, and another garden I had immediately adjacent to a gravel pit, have given me dreams of a different kind!

Sometimes if your house is new, your garden will consist of sub-soil. All the top-soil will either have been carted away or it will have been covered with the sub-soil bull-dozed from the foundations. If it is a heavy clay sub-soil, the top-soil having vanished, the best thing to do, regardless of expense, is to invest in several loads of top-soil. Like everything else, it gets more expensive every hour—the transport makes it costly—but think of the hours of labour you will be saved, and the cost of hours of labour if you employ professional help. Also, you will save on manure, peat, ashes, spent hops and all the other panaceas which you would have to resort to and dig into it, if you decided to tame the sub-soil clay. Make sure your top-soil is local. It is terribly easy in my part of Sussex to order top-soil which comes twelve miles away from the chalk Downs and which is completely different from the local acid soil. This is an expensive mistake I've made and vow I never will again! My rhododendrons had as big a headache as I did. If your builder *has* removed the top-soil, bully him to try and get it put back; it was *your* top-soil and you are entitled to it.

Whether your soil is acid or alkaline is most important, as this factor will decide the sort of plants you will be able to grow. All things in all, let's hope it is acid, as an acid soil will allow you to grow many more of the worthwhile plants. If it is alkaline, this is a challenge we will meet. 'How do I find out?' you are now saying, and here is how.

If you are a Fellow of the Royal Horticultural Society (and all keen gardeners should be, as not only can you see the Chelsea Show and all the other shows they hold monthly, but you can visit and learn from their own marvellous gardens at Wisley in Surrey), they will carry out a soil test for you if you send them a suitable sample. If you are not a Fellow you could have your soil tested by your County Agricultural Advisory Service for a small fee. This will give you what the pH value is. If you would rather do it yourself, go to your nearest seedsman shop or gardening centre and there buy a small kit for this purpose. It's rather like litmus paper when we did chemistry at school. The pH scale is a measure of acidity. An acid soil has a pH value below 7. An alkaline soil has a pH value above 7. As lime is added to your soil, so its pH value will increase. pH 5 is about the best for rhododendrons.

Sandy Soils

These are light, well aerated and easy to dig. They are free-draining and warm up quickly in the spring. Their disadvantages are that they lose moisture too quickly in hot weather and they lack soil nutrients. The cure is to feed the hungry brute with as much compost, peat, spent hops, farmyard manure, pig manure and as much fibrous material as possible to keep the soil open but also to hold as much moisture as possible. You will need to mulch a lot with a sandy soil (mulching will be described later).

Chalk or alkaline soil

These soils are too rich in lime. They also need abundant organic matter. This always rots quickly in chalk soils so they are always 'hungry'. Keep up the manuring and adding of humus of all kinds.

Peat soils

These are really very unlikely unless your little grey home is in the west or on similar soils. You will need to add chalk and 'marl' your soil. Lime must be added, and fertilisers of all kinds, as the soils are usually thin and lack nutrients—(there is no food value in peat by the way—it's a modern panacea for all soil ills, but always remember when you add peat you are but improving the nature and workability of your soil; you are not manuring it, as such).

Stony and gravel soils

These are similar in a way to sandy soils, only the granules of soil are larger and have often become stones! Such soils are usually thin and require humus in the same way. They do hold moisture a little better than sandy soils and for this reason only remove the very large pebbles to make your soil more workable, as generally the undersides of the stones form a reservoir of water for plants, and they also keep the soil cool. Small boys used to be employed by farmers a hundred years ago to stone the fields but it's a never-ending task in that the next time you dig or plough, up they come again like a crop of weeds.

Loamy soils

Like the one I had at the mill! There is sand and humus and clay all in a perfect blend like the best Scotch whisky. It's a joy to work; you will need manure and compost, of course, but not nearly as much. If your soil is like this you are in clover.

Clay soil

This is known as heavy soil and how sadly true such a description is. Sometimes after rain it is impossible to work. You are lucky if under your soil there is a sub-soil of gravel or sand, or some porous material but if your sub-soil of clay goes down several feet you will have to drain it with field drains (a kind of pottery pipe in 9 in. lengths) or you could on a new site fresh from the builders utilise the many broken bricks and rubble you will find. Make a deep trench of some 2 or 3 ft. filling the base with rubble, top up with ashes, then a few turves, then your top-soil. These trenches should lead from all over your garden to a 'soakaway'. Why it's so called I'll never know, because this, in effect, is where your water will be contained.

It should be about 10 ft. deep, 5 ft. across, and with the same content as the trenches, except that the rubble part should be about 4 ft. deep, the ashes 3 ft., then the turf and the soil.

For general treatment of a clay soil, my method is to drain if absolutely necessary. Break up your-sub soil, take away your clay top-soil and import a good garden loam from a garden centre. Expensive, yes, but it saves many a heartbreak and many a rupture!

If you are going to persevere with clay on the site you'll need to burn some. An enormous fire of wood is enclosed with clods of clay. After burning, the residue is friable and will help the texture of the remaining soil. Add ashes and humus of all kinds. I once bought a Georgian house with, I thought, the most marvellous loamy soil. It was a top-soil of compost, humus and pig and cow manure, added and worked for two hundred years. Any new addition to the garden we made there was the awful, virgin, Sussex wealden clay. So it is possible to tame clay. But who wants to spend two hundred years at the task!

Green manuring helps. Quite briefly, green manuring is either digging in all weeds—or sowing some member of the pea family, vetches, lupins or mustard (as a crop), and digging them in at the height of their lushest growth. The pea family is especially rich in nitrogen. Never burn the old pea haulms from a row of peas. Pull them up (you need the roots as they contain valuable nodes) and compost them or dig them in.

Compost, you see, is valuable for all soils and so I suppose I shall have to tell you how to make a compost heap, as if you didn't know already.

Compost and mulches

Let us make very sure of a 'do not' to start with—if you have used weed-killers on weeds and on the lawns, then such weeds and such lawn mowings should be burnt and not composted.

Make a lid-less box (with the earth as the floor of the box), of wood or corrugated iron sheets—about 3 or 4 ft. high. At the bottom place a layer of vegetable matter—weeds, grass cuttings, dead flowers, tea-leaves, potato peelings, vegetable and organic waste of all kinds—plus only soft wood cuttings, no hard wood. Then sprinkle on a proprietary compost activator, or sulphate of ammonia at the rate of $\frac{1}{2}$ oz. to the square yard plus $\frac{1}{2}$ oz. superphosphate also to the square yard, and cover with 3 in. of garden soil. Continue with layers like this until you have reached a height of 4 ft. (this will eventually shrink). The idea is that the heap should heat up, thus destroying weed seeds.

You will therefore water the heap in dry weather, and in very wet weather you will cover it so that it does not lose heat. Do not add dead autumn leaves to a compost heap as they will slow the process down. You should make a similar box for them with wire netting sides and leave them to rot down for a couple of years. In this case do not use an activator. Instead, you could use fresh farmyard manure. Poultry manure is a very strong, indeed dangerously strong, manure to use in a garden and should be only used after it has been mixed with a compost heap and left for at least a year. Then it is especially valuable.

If you are keen to get maximum growth, and for your new garden to mature as quickly as possible, then you must use composts and farmyard manures (cow, pig and poultry) in lavish proportions. It is my opinion that artificial manures give a plant a splendid stimulus, but they are not as lasting as an organic manure. Continual artificial manures will weaken and exhaust a plant and finally sour and leach a soil. You can never put into your soil too much organic matter and natural fertiliser. But here again, one must qualify—certain plants do best on a poor soil. And it is the getting to know what is right for what, which makes gardening such a fascinating hobby of continuing variety and complexity.

To mulch a soil is to cover it with a light coating of manure, compost, spent hops, grass cuttings, sawdust, etc. with the object of conserving moisture by evaporation. Never mulch in a very dry period. Mulch after rain to keep the moisture in. If you mulch in a dry spell when it does rain, the rain will find it more difficult to get to the roots of the plant. Mulching benefits the soil generally as it gradually decays and is absorbed in the top-soil. It also has the great advantage of smothering weed seedlings, and a good 4 in. mulch of grass cuttings continuously applied on a rose bed throughout the season will keep black spot from your roses.

I mulch a lot. I'm all for it. There is one disadvantage, and that is that birds will scratch about amongst it and sometimes will distribute it all on a lawn. If you are very much subject to this constant untidiness, then the beds you intend to mulch most should either be bounded by an easily swept path or, you should edge these beds with short box hedges, or perhaps hedges of santolina (cotton lavender) or dwarf lavender. Even an edging of pinks will help.

2 Count your Assets

We are now going to take a walk round our bare empty site, if we are creating a completely new garden; or our old and overgrown garden that we are to re-organise.

The first thing we must do, is to find out in which direction is due south and the other points of the compass. Due south is where most of your sun is to come from, and if you have a garden which slopes to the south you are the luckiest of all. If it slopes south-west the next luckiest, south-east the next—but if your garden faces due north you are surely the most unfortunate. Do not despair, however, we can cope no matter what your aspect.

Light is, of course, the most important 'ingredient' of a garden. More important than soil. It is the action of light on the leaves of a plant (photosynthesis) which creates the necessary plant foods, together with the food and moisture absorbed by the plant's roots which makes it grow. That's why plants in the country grow better than plants in the town. There is more light. Today air is cleaner in towns and some plants can grow in the centre of large cities today which would never have been able to years ago, which gives one hope over the pollution and conservation problems which face us. Again, in towns, *because* of the chemicals in the air, one often does not get black spot on roses; in the countryside, particularly near the sea because the air is so clean, one does. It's an ill-polluted wind, etc.!

So we know which way we face. Do we slope? I hope we do, because even if we don't we will have to create some different levels in our garden. If we are dead flat then we shall have to scoop out and build up with what we have scooped. If we are on a steep slope we must terrace it. That is to say, we must make a series of gigantic steps with small steps to connect the gigantic ones—or if we have slight slopes then we may make two separate levels with perhaps steps or a slope between.

Are there any trees? The whole look of your garden is so improved by the presence of mature trees but whereas the interior decorator can achieve an effect within weeks, a garden designer must have perhaps fifty years to produce the final effect with mature trees. However, there are quick-growing trees as well as slow-growing trees—and hedges, which will grow to 10 ft. in five years or so. It will help enormously if you can inherit a tree—or better still a group of trees—or if you were born under a lucky star, an avenue of trees. I do beg of you, though, do not cut any trees down; certainly not for the first years. No matter how shady it makes you, no matter how it drips on your washing, do not be precipitate in the destruction of a tree. Don't lop a great lump off it either, without any thought. This may be as bad. You may scar or disfigure a tree to such an extent that it is better removed anyway. I cannot understand why some Borough Councils or other local authorities will plant what were orginally forest trees by the sides of suburban roads and then proceed to pollard them until they are great trunks with a few thick branches with enormous blobs of wood on the end of each short, deformed branch, from which sprout for one year or perhaps two, a multitude of canes which flap against the top windows of passing buses.

You may have some old shrubberies. Don't grub them up until you have looked at the individual shrubs, sorted them out, and kept either what is precious and unusual or what takes a long time to grow. You may have to let light into an old shrubbery; and you may, when you re-arrange your levels, have to pile soil round an old tree. You must never raise the soil round an old tree for more than 6 in.—or a foot at most. The best way to cope—if cope you have to—is to bring your new level to within 2 ft. of the trunk of the tree and make a dry-stone retaining wall to hold the earth back from the trunk. Even then you will have to drain the little basement area you have created; otherwise it will fill and drown your tree. It could never live if it stood in a pool of water every time the rains came.

As you go round, have you a stream? A pond? A lake? You will be very lucky if you have. Especially a lake because, to a lazy gardener, a lake is just so many square yards he does not have to weed, or dig, or mow. To have water is a great blessing, and a blessing we shall provide ourselves with if we do not start off with it naturally.

Rocks, have you got? A fabulous view? Tumbledown buildings? Upright buildings, like picturesque farm buildings, could be incorporated into the gardens, as Lutyens did with the farm buildings at Great Dixter. You might even have parts of a mediaeval castle such as Vita Sackville-West had when she and Harold Nicholson wove round them the tapestry of Sissinghurst. All gardens should seem to grow naturally, and seem to belong to the site on which they are made.

You have by now decided on your assets. Some large trees, a view, some water, and a site which is either on different levels, or has the possiblity of different levels. You know its soil and what will grow with you or will not. You don't want to see all of your garden at once. If it is a suburban oblong, then you can so arrange it that we'll see part of it at a time. Some of it must be a surprise.

Let us, however, visualise the garden as an entity in our minds; our walk will be a succession of different pictures—we will go perhaps from a paved terrace, down some steps, through an arch covered by a flowering creeper to a lawn cut into rose beds—through the rose garden into a garden complete in its own right with yew hedges round it, a sundial in the centre as a feature surrounded by herb beds, surrounded by short box hedges, as in a knot garden of long ago. From this you will go through a topiary arch perhaps to a large empty area of lawn with curved borders of shrubs and trees round its extremities as in some woodland glade; the centre sunny area a close cropped and beautifully tended lawn. Each vista as it appears to you is a separate picture. In a large garden a succession of pictures, in a small garden one picture which may appear differently from differing angles as seen from the house or from the street.

Your garden, be it large or small, will have a boundary, and this boundary must be made with a hedge or with trees. If you need to make a quick growing hedge as a screen which also needs height, use *Cupressocyparis leylandii* but if you are not in quite such a hurry (and you can trim this one with impunity) use *Chamaecyparis lawsoniana*. These are good because they keep their same glorious foliage in all seasons (In the case of the *C. lawsoniana*, a bluey shade of dark green.) If you are on a windy site and need a high hedge then you must stake your *C. leylandii* well—it's not so much that they are shallow rooted, as that they grow so quickly above ground that they present a large area to a strong wind, and need support.

Being on a windy site makes your boundary hedge of great importance. Wind is very like water—if you stop it, it builds up behind the dam and then spills over in a strong torrent the other side—but, like water, if you filter it through, the filtration slows it down and disperses the strength of its flow. So a hedge on a windy site is really better than a wall, and a hedge that is not too impenetrable so that wind can get through it. Don't use yew as a wind barrier, use beech; for, although the brown leaves stay on the branches in the winter, they are not as thick a screen as an evergreen would be. If it is a wind coming in from the sea you will need to use tamarisk, berberis, *Euonymus alatus* (the spindleberry), *Senecio laxifolius* (most grey-leaved plants are happy by the sea), escallonia and *Olearia haastii*, both of which are evergreen. Smaller shrubs are fuchsia and hydrangea. Fuchsia, as visitors and natives of Cornwall, Devon and Ireland will know, makes a beautiful hedge; but hydrangea could hardly be called a hedging plant—but they would make an excellent screen, never to be trimmed by shears of course!

If you need to keep out cattle and animals, then hawthorn is the best hedging. Holly is excellent but it is slow growing. Hawthorn is fabulous for exposed positions and could not be hardier.

If you need formality and a sense of period, there is nothing better than yew. Now yew (*Taxus baccata*) is supposed to be a very slow-growing hedge and for this reason is often not used. But if I tell you that I planted a formal garden here in Sussex with yews of about 2½ ft. in height at the maximum, and after six years I now cannot look over them—and I am 6 ft. tall—then you must believe me. If you don't belive me then we are both wasting our time! These bushes were planted in November (this is a bit late for yews—I would rather have had them in when the soil was warmer), rather too closely, 3 ft. from trunk to trunk. I gave them a good wide trench with old turves in the bottom, then plenty of decaying humus from my wood, mixed liberally with some very old cow manure which I dug from the floor of an old barn—it was dusty and friable and very dry, but it mixed well. Old wood ash was also worked in and weeds were never allowed to grow amongst the bushes. I did not trim them at all for three years and then I just shaped the sides with the shears and the tops were lopped with the secateurs; this was done in August so that all the cuts had healed over by the first autumnal frosts. In my first garden I ordered fifty small yews. I did not prepare the ground at all (it was gravelly loam) and it was also a very exposed site. Half of them died and by the end of the three years we lived there, the survivors looked exactly the same as when I put them in. Let me give you a hint here which I may expound upon later on when we get to the actual planting of shrubs—or indeed the planting of anything. If you want a plant or shrub tree to really do well you will have its roots out of the ground for as short a period as possible.

As you unwrap its roots do not leave them exposed to the sun or wind (wind especially) for a moment. Sun and wind on the roots of a plant are most deleterious. Get those roots underground as soon as possible—get them into friable soil which will snuggle closely into and as near the tiny hair-like roots as possible, and make sure all the soil is touching the roots by giving a good treading-in of the soil around the trunk of the tree and above the roots. See also that those roots have plenty of room. Spread them out so that not only can rain reach a lot of them but so that they have as wide an area as possible to feed and to anchor the plant in the ground.

A newly planted yew shrub (indeed any shrub) must not be allowed to sway in the wind. If it does a funnel-like hole is made round the bole (sounds like an odd ode), down which too much air and water will flow and the plant will suffer. Also, if your yew shrub looks a bit seedy—i.e. its leaves begin to go brown, water it on every dry day (if possible twice a day), and water it all over with the rose on the watering can. Keep this up all the first summer and you will be rewarded, as I have been, with healthy, mature-looking yew hedges after only six years. In twelve they will look positively archaic! And never, oh never, dear reader, plant when the ground is wet and soggy. For this reason never dig the hole for your bush until you are about to put the bush in, otherwise it may fill with water and the roots of your bush will literally drown.

A point to remember with all hedging is that some hedges will need pruning. Some will need trimming only once a year and some will need trimming at least three or four times a season to look really neat. Privet—and I do like the sunshine of a golden privet hedge in a shady corner—needs at least three trims, whilst *Lonicera nitida* could often do with four. It's odd that this small-leaved, evergreen hedging shrub should be a honeysuckle. It doesn't have a flower and if you are going to grow it higher than 4 ft. it will need some kind of support inside, such as stretched wire or wire netting. Laurel is too greedy and in a small garden takes up too much nutrient from the surrounding shrubs and plants, but if you do have a laurel hedge *in situ* and you intend to keep it, for heaven's sake don't take the shears to it for trimming—this way you will get half-leaves and the whole effect is very nasty. No, use your secateurs and cut the actual branches under the leaves. It will take longer but it will not need doing so frequently. What about *Rhododendron ponticum* for a hedge? *R. ponticum* is the wild one with pale mauve flowers. It is very hardy—it will need to have room and will become quite wide (no shears here either). It also does well in shade and semi-shade, bit it must have an acid soil.

Thuja plicata is the best conifer for a lowish hedge and takes quite kindly to clipping. It will give a very neat appearance when trimmed but it needs protection by a polythene screen for its first couple of years in the winter if it is exposed to easterly winds.

Flowering hedges are becoming increasingly popular. For a loose hedge which is evergreen and flowers in drooping branches like a golden fountain and which smells deliciously of the most expensive after-shave, I recommend *Berberis stenophylla*. It is very prickly to weed amongst when young and you need to cut it back after it has finished flowering in late April. Then there could be rose hedges. The sweet briar rose grows quickly and can be trimmed to exactly the shape you want—on a wet summer evening the scent from it is redolent of all English summers in every sunny Victorian garden with crinolines bustling past croquet hoops. The floribunda rose 'Queen Elizabeth' is too tall for a rose bed (it's very lovely at the back of a mixed shrub border in a group of three—each allowed to grow 10 ft. high or more) and is often used as a hedge. It grows in an upright form and it is covered with beautiful, almost hybrid tea-like blooms for most of the summer. In very mild gardens it hardly loses its leaves in the winter and in most gardens for only a few weeks in the year. Bought in quantity it is not an expensive hedge and is certainly spectacular. I would advise you to use a short run of it only, as to have a suburban garden completely enclosed in a bright pink flowered hedge would inhibit the rest of your colour schemes. And remember with flowering hedges generally that most of the blooms will be on the sunnier side.

If walls are part of your boundary then you must clothe them—if they are of old brick or stone then you must not cover them completely but show the stone and brick at intervals through the plants. Choose colours of leaf and flower to blend with, contrast and enhance the colours of the wall.

I have enclosed part of my garden with a *Cupressus lawsoniana* screen. It is not trimmed and now, after six years, it is over 10 ft. high and at this height it has been stopped. That is to say the lateral tips of each tree have been cut off with secateurs and the screen will not be allowed to grow any higher. Now this is a satisfactory enough boundary. But I am the lucky owner of the field beyond, so behind it and about 10 ft. away from it and at 20 ft. intervals, I have planted about twenty standard flowering cherries of different varieties. These, after six years, have well-topped the hedge and I have a picture, first of my shrub and herbaceous border, then the screen and then, colourful in spring and autumn, the brightness of my row of cherries —all of different shapes and colours and beauty. But it is not everyone who is lucky enough to be able to plant, as it were, beyond his own boundaries. I suppose you could make a gift of some trees to a neighbour and tell him where to plant them and then enjoy them as if they were your own.

3 Near the House

The part of your garden nearest the house, that is to say the part you step out on to, is important and we will deal with it next. In its way it is neither house nor garden; it should be an outside room. Even in this uncertain climate of ours you should provide a sitting-out place. 'Patio' I will not stand for, it's so redolent of torrid heat and blue skies, but 'terrace' I will allow, even though, in some instances, it will be quite small, and 'a terrace' does sound a little bit Stately Home.

The terrace will be formal, possibly the most formal part of your garden, and it will be one step down at least from the door or french windows of the house. It will then extend ideally at least two-thirds of the height of your house and really should never be less than about 12 ft. wide. If the ground below your terrace is a much deeper level you will have to have steps down from it—make these wide enough for at least two people to walk down at once—narrow steps look rather mean. Also if the difference in height is 2 ft. or more you will need some kind of wall to finish off the terrace—and if it is a formal kind of house and the effect you require is a period one, then a balustrade is the best for this. Should you have a house later than Victorian —unless it is a Georgian style—then a balustrade will seem out of place. We do need to take great care all the time to make sure that the terrace at least belongs and is in keeping with the style of the house. The further we get away from the house the more free and more daring the design may be.

To determine the height of the terrace you need to peg out on the site the width and take levels at regular intervals—thus you will find an average level which will obviate your moving too much soil. When the soil has been shifted to form the flat terrace the surface should be levelled (sloping very slightly, 1 in perhaps 6 ft. away from the house to make sure storm water is not held against the side of the house). It is as well to mention here that the level should be such that any flower beds round the house should never have the soil sufficiently high for it to come to, or indeed to be within 3 in. of, any air bricks in the wall of the house. If you decide to have a formal pool on the terrace—and it is a very suitable place, for a formal pool and fountains are interesting features to watch from the house— then the hole should be excavated in the terrace now and the surplus soil taken out and used to extend the built-up area of the terrace. A stone retaining wall is best for the terrace as grass banks need constant upkeep. Even if the retaining wall is only a foot high it could be a dry wall with plants in it and the whole effect most charming. There should be a coping to the wall, a little higher than the edge of the terrace, to give a finishing-off effect. At the base of the retaining wall, no matter how high the wall, there should be a border with the width getting wider as the height of the wall increases. This border will house the roots of the climbing plants which will cover the wall and balustrading. Of course a short hedge of lavender or yew could be used instead of the balustrade and clipped to a formal outline.

The steps joining your terrace to the garden are of the utmost importance. Unless you are very cramped for space, the steps must never be steep ones. Also make them wide so there is plenty of room for a juvenile or elderly foot. The length of two bricks is a good width for the tread and the height of one brick is a good height for the rising part of the step. If you use cement for the steps make sure there are plenty of holes made for rock plants to grow from. There is nothing so raw looking as a flight of bright and new brick steps. Old bricks are always better in a garden as the remaining mortar always seems to help the moss to grow and to weather a brick. Similarly, plants growing from new bricks even, will soften the look of them and will encourage moss and weathering. Do not, however, plant strong growing subjects in your steps (what you want is dwarf thymes, etc.) as there is nothing more irritating or dangerous than to have to pick one's way down some steps over large cushions of vegetation, especially in the wet.

Also, do get expert advice about the hardness or frost-proof-ness of the bricks you use for paths. It is very disappointing, to say nothing of the extra labour and expense needed for re-placement, if you use bricks which the frost gets into and then cracks, shortly afterwards causing brick after brick to crumble and disintegrate before your astonished gaze. If you have a lot of straight lines on the terrace then circular or semi-circular steps might prove effectively contrasting. If you have more than a dozen steps in your flight then you must have a reason-able area half way as a landing.

There needs to be a considerable area of hard paving, either stone, brick or cobbling on your terrace as it is here where you will sit out. Also being nearer the house this is the all-weather part of the garden. One cannot, alas, determine what comes down from the skies but one can make it as pleasant as possible underfoot, by ensuring that this area is as quick drying as possible. Keep it fairly open; this will help the view of the rest of the garden. Also, with hard, and slightly sloping surfaces this area will dry out more quickly than other parts of the garden. If you are going to turf any of it (and this is a very pleasant thing to do) make sure this lawn is very well drained and is also fractionally higher than the surrounding brickwork as you can trim the edges more easily. There is nothing so difficult, time-consuming or temper-fraying than to have any grassed area just lower, or on a level with a hard surfaced path. Always a little higher please, and the long-handled shears will keep a trim edge quite speedily.

If your terrace is facing south and it is a fair size and not too overshadowed by the house, a sundial makes a very pleasant feature. Beds could then radiate from it. If it does not face south, some statuary perhaps but if you decide on a pond then a fountain is a must. If the fountain is worked by an electric pump then the proximity of the terrace to the house is a great advantage as you can have the switch inside the french windows. Then engage your guest in some witty badinage to distract his attention as you go out into the garden, at the same time flicking the electric switch with your foot to give the necessary picturesque effect. Let me add here that I think fountains which change colour because of coloured lights in your pool are unbelievably vulgar in a garden but are splendid on the promenade at Blackpool.

Instead of a retaining wall to hold the soil between your terrace and the level below, it is sometimes a good place to house your rockery. It is a good natural slope for the positioning of the stones in proper 'strata' form and the slope helps to drain the soil which is essential for a rock garden. I have used the area between my terrace and the lower level for a rock garden instead of a long retaining wall (I actually have both). I have wide brick steps which divide the rockery into two. This is one of my mistakes! I should have had stone steps of the same stone as the rockery and they should have had an informality about them as if they had been carved out of a rocky site; they should have meandered a bit as a mountain path does when it seeks a different level. To have a rockery in this position does save the amount of stone you would have had to use in a retaining wall, be it a dry stone or a cemented one. Whilst we are talking of rockery work it is essential that you use local stone. Local stone is the only one that looks 'right'. It is no good, no matter how rich you are, sending to Westmorland for stone for a Sussex rockery. If you are on a chalk area where there is no local stone, use stone from the nearest natural outcrop. Not only is it aesthetically more satisfying but the transport will be cheaper. Cost in gardening today is a very important factor. If you want a cascade of water down your rockery, and this is a very happy way of using water in your garden, then to have the rockery at the foot of the terrace means that you are near to the house electricity for the pump to circulate your water from the bottom of the pool to the top of the cascade.

Plate 1: The hazel wood in the spring

Plate 2 (*top*): Outside the potting shed in my Sussex garden, I
talk to my prize-winning English Setter Samantha, whilst
Jolly, the Cocker Spaniel, looks on. Henry, the Jack Russell terrier,
is out of sight digging up the lawn!

Plate 3 (*bottom*): This photograph shows the midden before we got
to work on it (see Plate 4 for the midden today). Corrugated iron
was replaced with shingle tiles and the woodwork renewed. The
corrugated iron roof on the open barn on the right of the picture
was replaced with old tiles, and the left-hand building taken down.
The whole yard was cobbled with stones from the beach at Mumbles

4 Outlook in all Weathers

It is easy to have a magnificent garden in June. 'A blaze of colour' says the proud amateur. But you have to live with and enjoy your garden for a whole year. It has to have certain enjoyable features which are static, like statuary, fountain, water garden, seats, paths, arches, architectural features of all kinds and interest. You proceed through trees and shrubs, some of which will vary according to season, and some of which will remain constant and beautiful throughout. Then, most difficult and demanding of all, you will have a succession of plants and interplantings so that there will be colour of a kind the whole year long.

The first thing a gardener learns is how short a flowering season most plants have and how, as soon as one particular flower is over, we must replace its lost interest with the next and the next and the next through the long gardening year. For this reason static and permanent points of interest are of great value. Also, if you have a lot of space, it is good to have a small garden, completely enclosed and on its own, of one particular kind of plant, hence the rose garden or iris garden. Another method, if your garden can only be divided a few times, is to have a spring garden, a summer garden and an autumn and winter garden. But if your garden is small we must accept the challenge and create a garden which will give us all-year pleasure.

Let us view this small garden from the terrace. We need a point of interest which will catch our eye and give us pleasure always. Our surest bet will be an evergreen specimen conifer; if it's a new garden a fairly quick growing one, and to give us sun during the dark days of winter: a golden tree. *Cupressus macrocarpa* 'Goldcrest' needs full sun and will be your quickest growing. It is a bright, sunny yellow, hardy variety, but needs staking well if it is on a windy site. *Chamaecyparis lawsoniana* 'Stewartii' is not only golden but it is beautiful in shape and fern-like in texture. It grows to about 5 ft. in seven years.

C. l. 'Lutea' is columnal in shape and has an open graceful appearance. The brightest of the three is *C. l.* 'Lanei'. All of these glorious golden trees need open south-facing positions and will also be the brightest in winter on their southern facing side. There are also golden prostrate junipers which, when established, will give you a pool of pure sunshine on the ground. *Juniperus communis* 'Depressa Aurea' is bronze in winter but in early summer as bright as a buttercup. Another is *Juniperus amedia* 'Pfitzerana'. (Both of them are good for hiding man-hole covers in a small garden.) A dwarf upright bush with shell-shaped sprays (say that quickly!) is *Chamaecyparis obtusa* 'Nana Gracilis'.

If your garden is sufficiently large then you could back the golden tree with a green one and a blue one. Yes, bright blue *Picea pungens* 'Moerheimii'. This is a spruce and is like a bright blue Christmas tree. There are low spreading ones, too, *Picea pungens* 'Prostrata'. In summer the new shoots of these last two are an almost Cambridge blue. But I will devote a whole chapter to conifers later on in the book.

Far from the house you could plant a specimen weeping willow; although deciduous, its graceful yellow pendulous branches always give pleasure in winter. Never plant it near to your house and never have it in a small garden because it grows so quickly and so enormously and such is the trans-piration of water from its vast leaf expanse, that there is no moisture at all left in the ground for other plants.

We are still contemplating and enjoying the view from the terrace. There may be one reason why you are not enjoying it. There may be what is known as an eyesore. A building, a distant pylon perhaps—you can do nothing about a near one— is constantly drawing your eye away from the more pleasant part of the garden view. What are we to do about it?

A quick growing screen. The quickest growing tree is *Cupressocyparis leylandii* and as it is evergreen then it will hide your eyesore both summer and winter. You could use Lom-bardy poplars but these are deciduous, that is to say their leaves drop in the autumn, but even so there is still a pretty thick tracery of branches and these can be thickened by a rambler rose twining through its branches. However you will have to wait a year or two before your tree is strong enough to support this. It will not help you in the winter, but in the summer, whilst it is still young, plant beneath it what used to be called Everlasting Pea (*Lathyrus sylvestris* 'platyphyllus'). This is a perennial plant and when established will rise to heights of

15 ft. or so. From a distance your poplar will appear to have pink or carmine blossom—and there is also a beautiful white variety called 'White Pearl'. Clay soil is best for these. Be careful when you plant your poplars though; because of their rapid growth they are surface rooting and are really unsuitable for a small garden and they should not be planted too near even your neighbour's building, no matter how much you hate it! Whilst I am talking about poplars, as well as the common Lombardy, there are the balsam poplars whose young leaves are very pleasantly aromatic: *Populus balsamifera*, whose buds are long, sticky and odiferous; then there is *P. balsamifera* × *trichocarpa* which is large, speedy of growth and has white-backed leaves and fragrant buds. Another is *P. balsamifera* 'candicans' which is medium-sized with downy twigs and known also as the Ontario poplar. The scent of a balsam poplar in the spring is very strong and exotic, and mine—I have three —were given to me as three cuttings about a foot high ten years ago—I transplanted them from my last garden after three years when the largest was about 3 ft. high and now they must be all of 20 ft. Poplars are not too fond of chalk, but moist clay they delight in.

Another quick-growing evergreen is *Cupressus macrocarpa* which is one of the parents of *C. leylandii*. It is the Monterey Cypress and it is not altogether hardy. The golden variety is hardier, the best cultivator being 'Goldcrest'. *C. m.* 'Lutea', also a golden variety, is hardy and good for the seaside.

You may decide to erect some trellis or make a rustic wood-work screen for your eyesore to hide behind. Rustic work (considered a little old-fashioned these days) is made from larch poles and will need renewing about every ten years or so. Trellis can be obtained in many attractive shapes and sizes and will be fitted as panels between either wooden or brick pillars.

To cover your screen you can choose from roses (climbing, pillar, rambling or old fashioned shrub roses), honeysuckles, ivies, or polygonum. The best honeysuckle for a screen is *Lonicera japonica* 'Haliana' which is evergreen and has smallish white/yellow flowers which are very fragrant indeed, especially in the evening. Mine climbed the side of a 20 ft. high house in two years and is a very vigorous creature trying always to envelope the whole and every summer anchoring itself to the window shutters which have to be freed every autumn so that they can be used to keep out the winter storms. The ivies are slow-growing and their flowers do not smell much, though they attract the earliest bees. The most picturesque—the variegated ones—are much sought after by flower arrangers. I recommend two kinds: *Hedera canariensis* 'variegata', and one which has quite large leaves of green and primrose yellow, *H. colchica* 'dentata variegata'.

Polygonum baldschuanicum is a hardy perennial climber (known also as the Russian Vine—I wonder why). This grows almost too rapidly—loses most of its leaves in the winter—and it bears clouds of the most attractive white feathery flowers in the summer and autumn. It's a wonderful plant for covering the top and sides of an oil tank, which is always placed by the central heating engineer exactly where it is most noticeable. They have a talent for this positioning; it wouldn't surprise me if they did not have to answer a question about this in their final qualifying exams—the most ingenious answer for the best eyesore gets the highest diploma!

The outlook from the terrace, or from the house of an old-fashioned suburban garden, used to consist of an oblong of lawn surrounded by four straight borders of flowers and shrubs with climbers or higher trees round the fences or boundaries. We must try our best to alter this, although, being an itinerant jester, I travel thousands of miles every year by train and see these oblongs by the million. If you want this sort of garden, start at least, by cutting it into two. Have a screen of some sort across the middle! But here it is best not to cut the garden into two equal halves. Also, don't make the lawn oblong; make it oval. Or make it almost oval. Make the borders have some very drunken curves. But definite, 'I-really-mean-it' sort of curves, still keeping your grass in the middle. Here, because you will see the first half from the house, will be your centre of attraction, statuary, sundial, group of evergreens. Now in the second half of your garden do not have an open space, but have the centre part a busy pattern of beds and flowers with a surrounding path with very narrow borders just big enough to contain the boundary hedge or the climbers of the surrounding fences or walls. This way you will achieve a view from the terrace, then, when you have explored that, you will go, as it were, into another room containing a myriad of beds, all of which will be treated differently with different plants.

If you step down from the terrace on to the lawn garden and then up from the lawn garden to the flower bed garden, or again down still further into this garden, you will have achieved variety of space and height as well. Then when I'm too old to tour any more and you have taken my advice all over the country, those awful oblongs will be no more and I shall not see them!

5 Grass

A lawn will be the background and the complement to the whole garden. It is green for the whole year. It will look well and well-tended in the drabbest months of all, and when all the flowers are vying with each other in every colour of the rainbow it will be the resting place for the eye, and it will take you, pleasant green magic carpet that it is, from one part of the garden to the other. The shape of it will vary—it is not necessarily on one level—it may slope—but in general level and texture there must be a uniformity.

Lawns may be part of a pleasure garden, or they may have specific uses like bowling greens, tennis courts or other games areas.

It is this ghastly climate of ours which makes lawns the envy of the world. If you would make your lawn the envy of your neighbours here are some helpful hints.

It is important to start well, to dig the site of your lawn well. Drain it if necessary and give it a good sub-soil and an excellent top-soil. If the lawn is to be formal, then levelling is the next important step. This can be done with the aid of a spirit level and a number of wooden pegs. If a lot of levelling is to be done beware that you do not remove the top-soil of one part and expose the sub-soil. If this is necessary, take the top-soil off, store it elsewhere in a heap, level the sub-soil and then bring the top-soil back. Use a long straight piece of timber as your straight edge and then put your pegs in about 10 ft. apart. Then level with the aid of the straight edge and spirit level.

Turfing makes a good quick lawn, but seeding is ideal as various kinds of seed are sold for the differing uses of the lawn, from the finest 'Cumberland Turf' used for bowling greens, to the coarser seeds containing rye for playing fields. Late summer, autumn and spring are the best times for sowing. You should allow the site to settle before sowing for a few weeks, as newly levelled ground needs to find its final level. Then check the levels and make good. Mark the lawn off into strips about a yard wide as you are about to sow so many ounces of seed per square yard. This is usually marked on the packet as it varies with the kind of seed, but about 2 oz. per square yard is the average amount. You need to cotton the seed bed to scare birds. Choose a dry day but make sure the seed bed is of a very fine damp tilth. After sowing use a finely-toothed rake to scratch the surface by about a half-an-inch. Scatter dry soil over the whole surface—dry mole hills are absolutely ideal for this—and then lightly roll. Make sure the surface is no longer damp or the seeds are likely to stick to the roller.

If the weather remains dry several days after sowing, you will have to water—but do it very gently with a very fine rose—don't pressurise all the seeds out of the ground. Remember only a gentle sprinkle.

Weeds will appear after about three weeks and so will the grass. Hand weed, walking very gently over the grass, and this gentle pressure, so long as it is dry when you do it, will help the grass. When the grass is an inch high you can lightly roll it. When it is 2 in. high roll again, and later in the day gently 'top' the grass with a very high set mower—$1\frac{1}{4}$ in. at least. It's got to be a sharp mower and it's got to be the right sort of day or you will, with a blunt mower on damp soil and grass, tear the new grass all out of the ground. Mow regularly from then on—frequently with the box off, so that the clippings will go back into the ground and help fertilise the new grass.

If you are going to turf a lawn prepare your ground in the same way—lay the turves as you would the bricks in a wall—in other words bond them so that the end of the second row of turves comes to the middle of the first row, this way you do not get one long straight join in any place across the lawn. Tread in each turf and use a plank to stand on. Work fine soil into the cracks. Remove the more blatant weeds as you lay each turf.

If you are to renovate an old lawn: hand weed and then use a lawn sand to remove the smaller weeds. Give a good top dressing of compost and fertiliser. If the lawn is water-logged insert drains. Also see to the level and, if necessary, take out whole turves with a turf cutter and insert sifted soil beneath. If you use a straight edge for this the light showing underneath will denote the declivity. If the edges of an old lawn are ragged —a foot from the edge cut a turf a time along the whole edge. Then turn each turf around the other way so that the newly cut good edge now is outside the lawn. Fill in the ragged edge with sifted soil and beat the newly laid turf well down. Sow seed on the bare patches and your new edge will be magnificent in a couple of weeks.

I never ever mow my lawn without cutting the edges. I would rather just cut the edges than just cut the lawn only.

There are hand mowers, motor mowers, rotovating mowers, petrol driven mowers, electric mowers with cables, battery mowers. There are mowers you can ride on. They can all be demonstrated at your local dealers or nursery and there are endless well-produced leaflets to entice you and to explain; as each mower is designed for a specific need and you know your own need and I do not, I'm disengaging my hand from yours now and letting you decide for yourself.

You will, however, need a turf-cutting half-moon tool, some long-handled shears—these are for edging—and some short-handled shears for awkward corners, but we will try never to have an awkward corner in your labour saving garden—in that case you can use them for hedges.

You will need a special lawn rake and a special lawn broom and I'll tell you why:

Beverley Nichols is one of today's most successful gardeners. Ever since he delighted us with his knowledgeable nonsense in *Down The Garden Path*, from his pen have issued charming and amusing essays on gardening. Many critics accuse him of being too fey and whimsical but who are they to decry someone who helps to brighten a drab world with great humour and charm. (Charm is an almost forgotten 'commodity' today.) But what those critics forget, and more than likely because of their ignorance, is the immense amount of gardening expertise which has gone into his books, years of successful gardening expertise which he is generous enough to share with his readers. Since *Down The Garden Path*, have come *A Thatched Roof, A Village In A Valley, Green Grows the City, Merry Hall, Laughter On The Stairs, Sunlight On The Lawn, Garden Open Today* and *Garden Open Tomorrow*. I had the pleasure of reading from three of these books on Talking Books for the Blind and I realised as I read them again, of course out loud, what delightful essays (almost Elia-like) these were, full of nonsense and humour and, above all, choc-a-bloc with gardening knowledge.

Now why have I gone on like this, suddenly, about Beverley Nichols in the middle of a chapter on lawns? Advisedly so. There is nothing perfect in my garden and one of the most imperfect things in it is the lawn. Whereas Beverley Nichols claims 'a perfect lawn'. So quite unashamedly I am going to give you a few words of his wisdom. He says incidentally, 'On my lawn there is not a weed, not a trace of a bald patch nor a blade of couch grass...'. How is this done? It takes time

—he says it took him four years. Quite quickly and without quoting he:

1. Gets rid of clover with a hormone weed killer, keeping strictly to the proportions advised on the tin.
2. Gets rid of moss by using a selective weed killer specialising in moss. And every spring he uses what he calls a 'scrabbler' which drags up dead grass and dead moss of course. It is a special fan-shaped wire rake.
3. He helps his lawn to breathe; constantly, as he calls it, 'dibbling' the lawn with a hollow pronged fork.
4. Fertilises the lawn. He uses a proprietary dressing which comes in two varieties, one for spring and summer and the other for the autumn.

Let us take for granted the constant mowing in the summer —and rolling with an old-fashioned roller now considered unnecessary because of the weight of your mechanical mower.

One must always remember that mowing takes an awful lot out of a lawn and for the lawn to grow and prosper this must be put back. I replace it with finely sifted compost and leaf mould mixed with a little sand, and this I distribute widespread like the Biblical Sower. If you use compost for this job you must make sure it has heated well—it's making sure that the weed seeds are destroyed, otherwise you will be distributing weeds all over your lawn. Come to think of it, perhaps this is why my lawn is so full of them!

It also helps to make your lawn soil acid and this helps the finer grasses to grow. This may be an old wives tale but I'm putting it in as it's one of the things one hears when gardening and remembers.

6 Paths—and Pergolas

Even if your garden is minute you will have to walk in it to get from one end to the other, either to stroll or to tend your plants. If it is a very small area you more than likely will pave it and have small beds and tubs for your plants with climbers going up on the boundaries. Such is the climate of these islands that you do need a hard surface for your paths, especially if you are to enjoy your garden in the winter—and I do hope you will be an all-the-year-round gardener.

Another point about paths is that they become part of the architecture of a garden in that they join it together, and the texture of the path, i.e. be it made of brick or gravel or grass or stone will give the garden its atmosphere.

The material selected for a path should harmonise with that of the house, its surrounding buildings and, for that matter, with the surrounding countryside. Paths are for walking on. It is an obviously fatuous thing to say, but do not therefore make your paths of slippery material. There should be no permanent puddles. Drainage of your path is very important. If your path slopes slightly and you have a foundation of clinker or ashes then that should be all the drainage required. Brick paths should be made on a 3 in. layer of sand, which again is on a porous foundation of clinker.

Gravel is not used for paths so much today as it was fifty years ago. If you have an old garden which needs re-furbishing then to do away with the gravel paths (which need a great deal of upkeep and weeding) might be a good first operation. A tar covering with suitable chips or small washed gravel would convert the old type gravel path into one of greater utility if not beauty. If it is to be a path of great length then this might be the best kind. Concrete paths are very utilitarian but are most ugly. If there are concrete paths *in situ* they could be covered in tar and chips or used as foundations for stone slabs or bricks. Crazy paving paths are also a little old-fashioned but with modern weed-killers can be kept tidily and are pleasing with the occasional rock plant here and there. (Mind the weed killer!)

The use of a grass path must be governed by the amount of traffic. A good width helps a grass path—a narrow one soon gets a worn track across it. If a grass path is going to get a fair amount of wear and tear, then the area must be cleared of turves, about 6 in. of soil removed, ashes or clinker put down and levelled, then a thin layer of soil added to cover the ashes, and the turves replaced. This way the path is well drained. If the grass path remains obstinately wet then you will have to put a land drain down one or both sides of it, too.

Natural stone of the area makes a first class path. York Stone slabs give a great feeling of opulence, which is understandable because it is so costly. York stone can be purchased these days from the platforms of disused railway stations, particularly in the north. There are many forms of manufactured stone slabs on the market and some of them are very acceptable. Choose the one nearest to the texture and colour of the local stone and never choose a very bright green, yellow or red. Paths and lawns are meant to complement the flowers, not to rival them with gaudy colours. There are some very nasty ones used round swimming pools today, and with that bright antiseptic and cosmetic blue water, what could be more hideous. You can make your own concrete slabs to exactly the size you need and colour the concrete as you make it to the shade you require, After they have weathered a bit then they do really look almost like stone. You can make your slabs about 2 ft. wide with 2 ft. wide squares of cobbles set in concrete to alternate in the manner of a draught board—this looks very pleasant and is very fashionable at the moment.

Brick paths are excellent and will weather to match any house or environment. They can be set in various patterns with an edge where the brick is on end. Herringbone patterns are effective. Make sure your bricks are hard enough to withstand the rigours of sharp frosts. Don't use a smooth brick; it is slippery and dangerous. Old bricks which you have cleared of mortar yourself—not too meticulously I hope—will be best because the mortar seems to encourage mosses and lichens and the bricks weather quickly. I have some steps which look centuries old and have been laid only five years.

Drives and courtyards and garage areas are too big to pave. I suggest you have a foot deep of hardcore well rammed in, over which you put some rough beach to fill in most crevices, then pour 3–4 in. of concrete (which arrives in those horrific lorries with the mixer working on top). This you level with the edges of planks, making a slightly serrated surface. Cover the whole with a thin layer of tar and washed gravel or small granite chips and you will have a drive to last you a lifetime. The colour of the gravel and/or the chips again must match the house, walls and other stonework in the garden.

It is sometimes charming to have a centre walk of brick or flagstones bordered each side with cobbling. Large stepping stones surrounded by cobbling are effective. Sometimes in a grass path it is effective to use stepping stones inserted in the turf to avoid wear of the grass. Or just a stepping-stone path in a wide border looks well and aids maintenance. This is useful in a rock garden.

A path must be kept level. If it is intended to be straight, do make it so; nothing looks worse than an almost straight one. To give a perspective to a small garden it is sometimes useful to make one end of the path less wide than the other with the sides converging, thus giving a greater effect of length, but your plants either side must play the same game or the effect is lost. If you are going to cheat do it properly!

Paths are important items to make firm decisions about early and to complete as soon as possible in your programme to assist the quick, further development of your garden. I would put boundary planting first, then the trees, which you need to get in because they grow so slowly, and then the paths.

Sometimes you may feel a path needs to be made to fit on to a building in an architectural way, or it needs near it some effective screening to hide an eyesore or to split one part of the garden from another. A pergola is just the thing. A pergola consists of piers of wood or stone or brick on either side of your path with cross timbers linking both across the path and down the length of it. Plants like roses, wisterias, clematis, honeysuckles, summer and winter jasmine, climbing hydrangea, etc. are then planted at the base of each pillar and a very lovely avenue and canopy of foilage and flowers soon materialises. It is best to have all kinds and varieties of climbing plants as you then have some flowers to enjoy throughout the whole season.

A very charming and effective pergola can be made of rustic work from larch poles but I prefer the more lasting ones of brick and timber. As I write that, I look up at my own pergola where I have one very drunken pillar, luckily much camou-flaged by an |'Albertine' rose, this defect being caused by my not making a sufficiently deep foundation of concrete on a rather damp clay patch. Your foundations need to be at least 2 ft. square and $1\frac{1}{2}$ ft. deep of concrete for a 10 ft. high pillar.

7 Levels, Walls and Rockeries

I would like to explore the ways and means of developing the various levels of a garden. I have discovered that to have a sloping site is an advantage. I'm not sure that it is an advantage if your garden slopes upwards away from the house. If it does so at a very steep angle and near to the house it will not only make the house dark but the house will make the garden shady. If it slopes upwards away from the house in a gentle slope then all is well and you will terrace it in the same way as if it sloped away but there is a very important job for you if the land slopes either steeply or gently towards your house, and that is drainage. Water always runs downhill and in these circumstances your house is acting a little like a dam. Drain each terrace to the sides and then drain the final area near the house so that your drains go either side of the house. If your slope is steep and there is a quantity of water then it would be a good opportunity for a cascade, having a pool on each level and then taking the surplus water from each pool to the next *via* a rocky canal. It sounds very grand and improbable but, in practice, the smaller versions of this kind of treatment are usually the most successful. If you are making your garden on several levels, it is therefore of paramount importance to drain.

I have mentioned earlier dry walls, which are an ideal way of retaining the earth in a terrace. They will not only do this for you but they also provide an ideal home for many rock plants— thus improving the design of the garden. Also this effective feature needs very little attention after it is built—the odd weed here or there, cutting off of seeds from the cushions of plants such as: dwarf achilleas like 'Argentea' and 'Tomentosa', *Alyssum saxatile*, arabis, armeria (thrift—new improved varieties), aubretia, dwarf campanulas, wall-flowers, and rock roses (cistus). I greatly favour the grey-leaved plants, all kinds of dianthus and *allwoodii*, erigerons (there are some good red ones now as well as mauve and blue), *Gypsophila repens*, which is only 4 in. high; variegated ivies, already discussed, would grow from the bottom of your wall upwards. *Hypericum repens* and *reptans,* iberis (that whiter than white perennial candytuft), linaria (toadflax), *Lithospermum prostratum,* sedum (stonecrop); sempervivums of various kinds, including the houseleek which on a roof brings luck to the householder, so much so that the Emperor Charlemagne passed a law to the effect that everyone had to have one. Thymus—I love the silver lemon-scented one—and veronicas. Lavender would be a good subject for the top of the wall. Dwarf nepeta (catmint) could be used in or on top of the wall. *Cotoneaster horizontalis*—fan-like and fishbone-like—would do well at the bottom of the wall. Small bulbs like crocus and snowdrops (which incidentally you move just after they have finished flowering) can be dibbled in under the lavender at the top of the wall, as well as *Chionodoxa luciliae* and *Scilla siberica.* If your wall faces due south and the lavender at the top gives shelter then under the lavender you could grow *Iris histrioides* for flowering in January and *Iris reticula* for a little later. But you can only plant these where the sun will really bake the soil for the rest of the year.

But before we give ourselves the joy of growing flowers in January we have to build the wall first. You will need for the whole length of the wall a good foundation of ballast and cement. Dig out a trench a foot deep. Bang into the bottom 6 in. of some broken bricks, stone or rubble. Bang it in hard. Then add 6 in. of concrete level with the ground of the lower terrace. Then on this build your wall of stone, artificial stone or brick, preferably stone. Put the biggest ones along the bottom course finishing with the smaller, flatter stones at the top. The wall must be battered. That is to say the wall is not built vertically but with a slope towards the bank it retains. Each stone will, as it were, lean inwards and you fill in the earth behind it. And like a brick wall you will have alternate rows of headers and stretchers. The join between the stones of one row will have a stone laid across it in the row above and below like bricks in a wall. As you build so you must plant. Lay the roots of the plants carefully in the crevices of the stones with their roots behind the stones so that they are able to fasten for food and security in the bank behind. You don't want to cover all the wall with plants, and in years to come every spring, or early summer rather, when a lot of the plants like arabis and aubretia have started to seed and the clumps have got really large, then is the time to take your shears, not just to the seed-heads but to the whole plants as the more vigorous will hide the more delicate and bashful. If your dry wall faces south you should have a flower border in front of it for here will be one of the warmest and driest parts of your garden and here you will be at your most daring and will put the early things and the precious things. For this reason don't make the border too wide so that you can keep your eye on what is going on and can shelter, cosset and feed.

To get from one level to the next, as it were, down your dry wall you will need steps and I've already touched on these. Make them bold, make them a feature and leave the odd hole or two for very low growing plants. At Hidcote in a flight of steps just under those glorious domed, stone, summer houses, they have planted very small bushes of *Cotoneaster horizontalis* right along the whole length of each step, snug against the riser. As the step is wide this makes a very beautiful effect. This is one of the joys of travelling round and seeing the Great Gardens—do not be put off by the fact that they are acres and acres in extent and you have a backyard. There will be some single thing which you will make a note of—do write it down at the time in full, otherwise you will try to decipher some garbled pencilled scrawl when you get home and will not remember what it was that enchanted you: the positioning of one plant against another so that you said to yourself, 'That's perfect!' It could be just as perfect in your small garden. And of course the big gardens have so many flowers you have never seen before, and must have. I personally cannot see enough of the great gardens. Don't just go once, go at two or three different times of the year—that is when you will appreciate the cleverness and the artistry of their creators.

I am not a rockery man myself. I have not the time as yet to devote to the weeding and the cosseting and to give the care that the true alpine rockery requires. Even so, I don't think a garden is complete without one. If you have a small garden, then so contrive that, out of some corner of the lawn comes, quite naturally, an outcrop of rock. The cost of stone and cartage has made the cost of large rockeries almost beyond reach, so not many people are going to have large rockeries anyway. Alpine plants can be grown very successfully in peat beds, which are roughly raised areas of peaty soil contained by low walls of peat blocks. Easily built and easily maintained as weeds are pretty allergic to peat—this is the best way to have what, in effect, is a rock garden on the cheap.

It is terribly difficult to set down hard and fast rules and directions for making a rock garden as so much depends on the site and the shape of the ground (this with the aid of the modern bulldozer to be hired at so much an hour, complete with operator, should cause no dismay these days. Mountains can be conjured out of molehills in no time), and the nature of the stone. Here are some sensible hints:

1. Choose a sunny position. Most of the true alpines like sun.
2. You must have slopes and contours in which you will insert your stones as if they formed a natural strata. Do not dab a stone here and there on a 'sand-castle' of earth like almonds on a cake.
3. There will be no straight lines. Bays and curves—why not make your miniature cliffs and mountain sides on either side of a winding path—the path to be of stone—or of stepping stones in peat, or earth, or grass.
4. When you set a stone in your slope, the side or end of the stone in the earth should slope so that water runs off the stone away from the viewer. Most stones should show about half, the rest, most wastefully, should be in the earth. You can cheat on this—but make it look that way! Great attention, however, must be paid to the stratification of the rocks. If you don't know what I mean by this, look at pictures of 'strata' in geological books in your local library. Look at pictures of rockeries and visit other gardens and your local parks and see how there is a kind of line—with each stone laid in its natural 'bed' or 'course'.

Now for the plants—you could use all the plants mentioned in the following list for dry walls. Achillea—'King Edward'. *Aethionema cordifolium*, variety 'Warley Rose'. *Alyssum saxatile*, variety 'Dudley Neville', which is an orange-yellow form. *Androsace villosa* and *Androsace helvetica*, *Anthyllis montana*. *Anthemis cupaniana*—this is lovely but very invasive—the foliage smells wonderfully after rain but its flowers smell 'orrible. *Arabis albida*, variety 'Flore Pleno'. Armeria or thrift, a deep purple variety called 'Vindictive'. *Astilbes chinensis* for a damp pocket. *Asperula suberose*. Aubretia comes in varieties which are pink, red, violet and blue and a double one called 'Barkers Double'. *Celonisia coriacea* which is a white daisy flowering from grey leaves. *Campanula carpatica, Campanula cochlearifolia* which is blue and there is a white one called 'Alba'. *Dianthus allwoodii alpinus* come in many named varieties and flower all summer through. Gentians; there are a myriad of these; *G. acaulis, G. lagodechiana, G. septemfida* and, for a shady spot, *G. sino-ornata, G. verna. Inula acaulis,* and the edelweiss

Leontopodium alpinum. Then next you must have *Lithospermum diffusum*, 'Heavenly Blue'; *Phlox douglassii*—variety 'Eva' is pink, Snow Queen is white and Violet Queen, violet blue. Some of the tiny primulas, like 'Wanda', are not really right for the rock garden, but I like them. *Potentilla nitida* 'Rubra' is like a miniature shocking pink geranium. There are a multitude of *Saxifraga*, silvery ones, cushiony ones and tiny mossy ones but you must go and choose them for yourselves. There are many kinds of sedums too, *S. caticolum*, with blue-grey leaves and a red-leaved one called 'Ruby glow', which I have in my herbaceous border, but it's only 9 in. high. I can also recommend *Sedum roseum*, *Sempervivums alpinum* and *S. glaucum*. A plant which I once saw most spectacularly growing is a *polygonum* alpine 'Donald Lowndes'—it flowers from May to October, but not with me, and I so wanted to have an opulent clump like the one I saw. There are tiny violas particularly 'Tricolour' with yellow and mauve faces.

Then you will need shrubs for your rockery. Let's deal with dwarf conifers first. The following are chosen because they will not grow more than a foot or so in ten years, but this rate of growth will depend enormously on their situation and how you feed them.

Abies balsamea 'Hudsonia' is slow growing, hardy and has deep green leaves and, like all fir trees, has bright new spring foliage.

Cedrus libani 'Sargentii' can be used almost as a trailing plant over a rock. *Chamaecyparis lawsoniana* 'Minima Aurea' is a small golden bush, *C. l.* 'Minima Glauca' is not very blue, *C. l.* 'Pygmaea Argentea' is silvery. *C. obtusa* 'Nana' has whorled fan-like foliage and is very slow growing. And for a little mound of dark green, *C. pisifera* 'Nana'. For a similar golden mound *C. p.* 'Nana Aureovariegata', with a name much larger than the shrub! *Crypotemeria japonica* 'Spiralis' will spread itself in a feathery irregular way over the rocks, best used on top of one of your miniature mountains!

Juniperus communis 'Compressa' is a tiny conical bush and it hates being moved (at least mine did) so make sure you are putting it where you want it. *J. horizontalis* 'Glauca' is a blue carpet but it needs room and is best used at the end of a rockery so that it can spread over the path or the whole of the tennis court! It is steel blue.

Picea abies 'Gregoryana' is like having a green immovable hedgehog in your rockery. *Picea mariana* 'Nana' is grey-blue.

A slow-growing pyramid form of golden yew is *Taxus*

Plate 4: The midden today. See Plate 3 for its original appearance.
It is difficult to imagine how the photographer managed to take this
picture without showing the surrounding beds, which are a mass of
all kinds of flowers (hollyhocks, delphiniums, lupins, dahlias, sedums,
geraniums, gloriosa daisies, pinks, hebes, buddleias, pyracantha,
roses, iris, alyssum, balm, verbascums, asters of all kinds, various
annuals, border carnations, etc. etc.). He did so, in fact, in order to
show how a dove-cote can be a splendidly decorative feature

Plate 5: This is where the drive (gravel chips and tar on concrete) meets the open courtyard before the house. Left, is the retaining dry wall about 5 ft. high, built from the old stones of the house. This runs along the whole of the north side of the courtyard in front of the house and is an example of how different levels become a feature

baccata 'Pygmaea Aurea'. I have it and in six years it has possibly grown half an inch. It's exhausting to watch!

Two more golden shrubs are *Thuja occidentalis* 'Rheingold' and *Thuja orientalis* 'Aurea Nana'. Also goldish, in that it is dark green with gold tips and globular, is *Thuja plicata* 'Rogersii.'

With such a plethora of plants and conifers when we come to the dwarf shrubs you will be ready to cry 'desist'! The point to remember is that unless you have an enormous rockery you will not want them all and a lot of your choice will be restricted by that awful cry of the nurseryman, 'Not in stock!' So you need an alternative suggestion. And also you will need with your nurseryman's aid to choose the right plant for the right soil and aspect. If he is knowledgeable, and most of them are, and if he desires to please and for you to come again, and most of them do, he will say things like, 'Oh no Mrs Feather, you are a bit too damp and acid to have a so-and-so. Why not have a such-and-such which is similar to look at but revels in acid and damp?'

Here are some shrubs for rockery. Not too many to confuse you. There are lots of dwarf evergreen rhododendrons and azaleas and the best thing is to go to a nursery in spring and get them flowering in containers. They grow slowly and are magnificent—always providing you are not on chalk. A tiny early blue one is R. *impeditum* and its variety which is mauve, 'Pygmaea'. This has glaucous grey leaves—there is Prostigiatum, a dwarf shrub of dense habit. The 'Kurume' evergreen hybrid azaleas would not be too large for some rockeries.

Dwarf brooms are lovely—*Cytisus decumbens* is prostrate, and spreading itself out in a generous shower of pale yellow blossoms is *C. Kewensis*. A near relative is *Genista pilosa*. *Genista lydia* is a dwarf broom with arching stems of golden flowers which may spread up to 6 ft.—with me it has spread less than a foot in five years. *Genista hispanica* is the Spanish gorse and it's about 4 in. high at most, forming dense prickly mounds covered with masses of flowers in May and June. I ordered two from a very reputable nursery which advertises regularly in the *Journal of the Royal Horticultural Society*. He sent me two bushes of common gorse which I thought were wrong and placed in my rockery. They are now about 5 ft. high and whenever I decide to remove them they cover themselves in glorious scented bloom and I have not the heart to. Besides, they are unbelievably spiney. *Genista tinctoria* (which is known as Dyers Greenweed so you know what fun you can have with this) has a lovely variety for the rockery, 'Plena'. It is semi-prostrate with double flowers.

Cistus—the 'Sun' roses—need full sun. There is *C. atchleyi*—dwarf and dome-like with white flowers. *Cistus* × *pulverulentus* (Warley Rose) has vivid cerise flowers and sage-green wavey leaves. I have it and it needs room. It's not on my rockery, it's in front of a shrubbery which is the best place and I really should not have mentioned it here but it's one of my favourite plants.

There are tiny roses—*Rosea chinensis*, which gives flowers later in the year when the first flush of spring is over. There is variety 'Minima' with single or double pink or red flowers.

The veronicas—they call them hebes now—from New Zealand are worth considering for the rock garden as they flower in mid and late summer. N. 'Bowles' Hybrid' has mauve-coloured flowers, *H. albicans* has glaucous foliage, white flowers and is very hardy; some hebes are not hardy everywhere so don't be distressed if you lose one or two. *H.* 'Carl Teschner' has violet flowers in June and July. *H. ciliolata* is a miniature hebe, and *H. edinensis* is suitable for the rock garden. The last hebe I shall mention here is *H. venustula*, which has white flowers all the summer and yellowish-greeny leaves.

8 Garden Features

Pots, Statuary, Sundials Dove-cotes, Well-heads and dare I say it, Gnomes

You will always need focal points in parts of your garden; they may form centre pieces for a separate garden—they may indeed be there in the form of a well, or you may need to be reminded of your mortality by a sundial. These items like statuary, or pots on a terrace, are particularly valuable in the winter as items of interest to draw the eye from the bare earth and the bare branches and the mass of decaying foliage you have had to leave round your tender plants to preserve them from the frost. Indeed, if your urns and pots are of terracotta and your statues of marble, then they too will only catch the eye because they are hideously swathed in polythene and straw to keep out the frost!

But seriously . . . if you have divided your garden into several parts you will need a focal point in each. Terraces will need pots or troughs. A rose garden or a herb garden will need a bird bath or a sundial or an astrolabe, whilst a dove-cote is best in a yard, midden or courtyard so that the doves can sun themselves on roofs—preferably white doves against warm red and lichened tiles. Statuary is best against dark shrubs; yew will give the necessary old-time atmosphere.

Plants in pots or tubs or troughs will need constant attention. They will dry out very quickly to start with. They must never be allowed to look untidy, dead leaves must be removed, plants must be properly and discreetly staked, if on a windy site. Because you have drawn a lot of attention to the plants by putting them in pots you must make sure that they grow on without hindrance so that they are the best plants of their kind. Foliar feeding and liquid fertilisers must be constantly applied and, very important this, *never stand a pot or tub in a draught*. It is important that your pot or tub should conform with the rest of the house and terrace. If your house is Georgian, your pots must be also, ditto Victorian. Tubs are pretty ageless and can be used almost anywhere. I prefer them painted white, green being my second choice. Do not, I implore you, paint them blue or red or yellow—these are gay holiday Mediterranean colours and not for these more subdued climes, and the bright colours detract from the flowers. A jeweller does not make his ring as bright as his gem.

You can buy—painted white—classical square hardwood tubs for orange trees for your terrace—with delicious decorative obelisks to match and suddenly your terrace will expect the dainty foot of Madame de Pompadour to light upon it! These are costly conceits, but not expensive when you consider the exacting period design and craftsmanship put into them by a firm called Anthony Manley of London S.W.6.

You can get all kinds of statuary at all kinds of prices and made of various materials. If you are very wealthy you can, and I hope you will, purchase an antique piece culled from some garden of yesteryear. It will set you back an awful lot, but the atmosphere it will give your garden will be beyond price. Site it well. The siting is almost as important as the statue you choose. If your vista is a long one, then the statue must be large and its size increased by a suitable plinth—it's no good looking down an alley of pleached limes a hundred yards long to see a dwarf marble Eros ploughing through the long grass. In a similar way, it is no good turning a sharp corner in a small yew garden to be suddenly confronted with a herculean soldier three feet taller than you are, prodding you with a raised trident. Don't have a lot of statuary either unless your place is vast. And don't be afraid to purchase one made from cast cement or reconstituted stone as, once weathered with moss and lichens, they look very well indeed. Incidentally a paint made from water and cow manure and applied with a whitewash brush will attract mosses and lichens to statuary, balustrades and all garden ornaments of stone or artificial stone. It is well worth while and well worth bothering a local farmer for.

I am an old-fashioned person, as you may have noticed from my jokes on the radio, and I'm afraid I cannot enthuse over modern statuary. I could not bear to see a view of part of my garden framed through a highly polished hole about two feet wide scooped out of the middle of a pin-headed lady who is entitled 'Maternity' and who looks, poor misshapen creature, like a seal that has so recently emerged from her native element, that she is dripping wet and about to shake her bronze (brazen too) self, dog-like (to mix a metaphor) all over you. Also, I am glad that I cannot afford to buy one of those out-of-space masses of rock which are ostentatiously mounted on (quite attractive) plinths and left in the middle of a lawn to remind one of the fact that this is what the world will look like if the pollutionists (is there such a word?) are allowed to exist much longer.

At the other end of the scale, I am most allergic to those diminutive sprites of a subterranean race in their pointed red hats and red waistcoats and yellow knickers guarding the treasures of the earth. Mass-produced nightmares they are to me. And the one that irritates me to positive madness is the one who sits fatuously smiling over a pool with a fishing rod and line, giving nervous breakdowns to the goldfish.

But if I frown on gnomes, I smile serenely on pigeons. Live ones especially. What is more beautiful than a flight of pure white fantails—perhaps a dozen of them flying against a blue sky with early morning sun on them? Gold one moment, and the next their whiteness becomes mother of pearl, and although so white against the blue of the sky when turning and rolling in their flight, in shadow the white itself becomes a blue dove-grey. This the glorious trick of sunlight on fur and feather. In the early light of an April morning the feathering of my English setter with the sun behind her becomes silver tracery. The soft, silky sound as the doves fly past you and the whirr of their pinions as they alight; their clear-cut cleanness; their utter white innocence; the charm of their courtship with their flamboyant tails and proud pouting chests; and the clean pink coral of their tiny feet are all sheer delight. Even the cooing of them soothes, and the whiteness of them against the red of a tiled roof on a winter' morning makes it seem like spring.

I once had two pairs given to me by the late Edward Seago, the artist. To stop them immediately flying home, you must keep them netted in for at least six weeks because, by then, they will have started nesting. This we did, but one yearned too much for Norfolk and made for home—from the remaining three we had eventually as many as thirty, and then nature took a hand and culled some with coccidiosis. We fed them with handfuls of corn and pigeon grain mixture—the rest they got from the free range of my grazing fields, garden and kitchen-garden and never once did they destroy seedlings or green-stuff, flowers or fruit. Their manure, when used sparingly, mixed with the compost heap, gave more advantage to the garden than they ever took out of it. This may not be the same in small suburban gardens but in the country they were faultless—give them some old mortar to peck amongst and they will not even eat your house! They must have this, and grit for their shells. I will not tell you the whys and wherefores of keeping them—any handbook on pigeons will do that.

Twice a year you whitewash the inside of the cote and once a week you clean them out. When making your cote remember pigeons need plenty of fresh air. They sweat through their breathing and not their skins. They breathe fast to oxidise their blood and maintain the high temperature in their bodies. When mine overstocked the tiny cote I gave them, I hung another spacious cote on a stone barn wall about twenty feet away from the original cote, which was the central feature of a cobbled yard, but they would never use it. Instead, heartbreakingly, they would roost outside on the roof of the cote and I would see them, when I arrived home at one in the morning after a late cabaret, shining with white frost in the moonlight, and in the headlights of my car.

O beautiful fantails! How we loved you. Now I have an English Setter dog and a dove-cote. But, being a bird-dog, she would be driven mad if I had real, live fantails again. And so would they. So in my mind's eye I see the flights of white doves I had years ago, and on my red tiled roofs I now have white china doves—exact replicas which shine exquisitely in the sun —or in the frost at night. The Chinese, I read once (I don't know if they do now, with their dedicated and regimented earnestness and their blue uniformed overalls), tied little musical instruments to their doves, which, when they flew, gave off magical fairy music. This must have been very lovely for the Chinese Mandarin in his garden below and a little frightening for the doves—but in a way there seems in this contrivance some similarity to the man who likes red, green, blue and yellow gnomes fishing in little ponds.

Dove-cotes are a beautiful feature in a garden. The actual dove-cote can be beautiful in itself and would not be beyond the capabilities of a gardener-handyman to make at home. You need several compartments which are quite separate and which have their own front doors, and which need a reasonable platform around them for the alighting and promenading of the doves. Also the height of the pole on which the dove-cote rests has to be the correct height in proportion to the size of the cote. Thatched ones are very pretty. Shingle tiles (i.e. wood tiles) are more lasting and less bother. The height of the pole is about seven times the length of the actual little building at the top.

Stone troughs are a fashionable ornament these days and a boon to the old, the invalid or the infirm. Stone sinks have been removed from kitchens to be replaced by steel or plastic ones— galvanised iron feeding troughs have replaced the stone ones on a farm and many a stone sink or trough is lying idle in some garden or farmyard corner. The idea of the trough is that in it you can grow the tiniest plants and know where they are. Raised 3–4 ft. off the ground the trough brings the miniature garden nearer to you without undue bending over or peering. It is, in short, a myopic's dream. You aim at a miniature garden within the bounds of your trough.

Having got your trough, make sure it has a drainage hole in it. Put a layer of coarse gravel or beach on the bottom, then loam mixed with peat, and some stone chips on the top after you have planted your plants. Miniature trees (bonsai), tiny conifers and miniature bulbs are all excellent. Try gentians and alpine pinks. Try hardy cyclamen—*C. coum* and *C. neapolitanum*. Other plants you could use are, *Anacylus depressus, Androsace helvetica, Campanula cochlearifolia* 'Alba', *Dianthus gratianopolitanus, Dionysia aretioides, Gentiana verna, Gentiana saxosa, Gentiana sino-ornata, Iris lacustris, Iris verna, Lewisia howellii, Linum elegans. Lithospermum oleifolium, Penstemon fruticosus, Phlox amoena, Potentilla aurea plena. Saponaria caespitosa, Saxifraga apiculata, Saxifraga longifolia, Saxifraga lingulata, Saxifraga oppositifolia splendens, Sedum acre, Sempervivum arachnoideum, Sempervivum montanum, Veronica prostrata*—and many more, but that, surely is enough for a sink! And you might be best advised to plant them in the spring rather than the autumn.

Well-heads look their best in cottage gardens if they are of brick with a thatched roof across the winding gear. There is no need for an actual well, but if there is one, of course, it's more fun. There is no reason why a brick well-head should have the customary roof of tiles or thatch; you could yourself design a large hoop of wrought iron, a little like those the stone Italian well-heads have, and get your local blacksmith to make it for you. Do try and get an estimate out of him first because these items can be very costly. Then, from places like Crowther of Syon Park, you can purchase very elegant and very costly (rightly so) original stone Italian well-heads—the largest making important points of interest for the middle of a large courtyard in front of a house for your Rolls-Royce to glide majestically around!

9 Shrubberies

There is something rather Victorian about the word 'shrubbery' you immediately envisage endless vistas of laurels, privets and *Rhododendrons ponticum*, dark and sooty with seedy laburnums and hollys. Today, however, there are so very many different shrubs and trees available, not only the species but endless improved hybrid varieties, that one does not really know exactly how to begin. In Hilliers', of Winchester, *Manual of Trees and Shrubs* compiled in 1971 as a catalogue of all the trees and shrubs they sell, they give brief details of over 8,000 plants representing 631 *genera*. This is an almost unbelievable range of trees and shrubs contained in one firm's nurseries. With this number in one nursery how do I start to pick and choose, advise and admire?

There is one easy division to start with. Some will only grow on acid soil and some on calcareous soils. Then there are many which are too tender for all parts of the country and some too large for all but the largest gardens. I will keep these to size, and try to recommend plants which will grow in all parts of our island climatically.

There are trees and shrubs which are to flower or be at their best in spring, summer, autumn and winter, and this might be a good way to divide them, for you, too. One might also make some suggested groupings for specific sites.

One point to remember is that shrubs are more permanent than other plants. They will grow in the same spot for many years, so in planting them you must make sure that they have room to grow to their full size. Be careful over the positioning of vigorous growers next to slow growers; make sure the positioning of the plants is suitable for it, i.e. if you have a Mediterranean-type plant be sure it is in full sun and has good drainage, whereas if a plant is a woodland plant in its natural habitat, make sure it gets shade; don't for instance, put two red foliaged plants together—plan both the texture and colour of your shrubs to show each off one against the other. In short, you must make a plan with pencil and paper and have an india-rubber ready to amend your jigsaw as you go along.

Your aim is to weave a tapestry of shrubs which will give you pleasure for a long time. Choose every plant carefully, make sure it is planted as well as possible to have every advantage, and ruthlessly adhere to this golden gardening maxim that, if in spite of reasonable care, a plant will not grow in your garden, get rid of it and grow something that does. That way the sickly one in a border which draws the eye inexorably, will be replaced and the whole will be a *pleasurable* whole.

Shrubberies these days are very seldom for shrubs alone. Some shrubs are used in mixed borders in conjunction with herbaceous plants, bulbs, bedding out plants and even annuals. Some shrubberies have smaller herbaceous plants used for edging, or to create bays of coloured plants to create interest for a longer period. I'm not at all pedantic myself, and unless you have an enormous garden there is joy in mixing other plants with the shrubs, using your shrubs as the backbone to the picture. They are the permanent members of your scene, which you can vary at will. Purists no doubt are raising their hands in horror, indeed some of them may have closed the book with a snap. But I am here as a keen amateur and must tell you how I break the rules—there is no need to follow me.

Shrubs can be arranged as borders. They can also, in effect, be island beds. Usually they act as a background or screen to stop you looking at all of the garden at once. They may form the theatrical back-drop to some water or other feature.

Before you start on your shrubbery, make a list of the shrubs and trees you would like to have. Visit your local parks, watch television programmes (especially mine), go and visit the great gardens—there are bound to be some near your home—at various times of the year, and make a rough list, no matter how long, and make your preferences. Deciduous plants, evergreens and conifers all must be included in your list. Every person will make a different selection, as personal choice always varies. This is one of the advantages a keen amateur has—he can make his own choice instead of bringing in a professional landscaper. Mark you, he will make many a costly mistake that the professional will not!

Having made this list of preferences, read up about the various species and hybrids and where their natural homes were originally. In your mind know their history. Then you will know which are the sunlovers and the shade lovers; the lime lovers and the acid lovers—you will find out which ones grow quickly and which slowly—which plants last forever and which ones need renewal every few years from cuttings—which are hardy or delicate. Thus a winter's reading will prepare you for a spring planting and a summer's enjoyment.

Your most useful shrubs will be the ones which give you decorative foliage—either all the year or all the summer, as well as having a flowering season. Add scent and hardiness to this as well and you have a star performer. Some shrubs you will only have for their foliage (like the *Acers*) and some you will have for their blooms only like lilac (*Syringa* is the botanical name for lilac, and the Mock Orange Blossom which is known as 'syringa' is the *Philadelphus*—which is an old Greek name for a sweetly-scented flowering shrub). One of the troubles of lilac is that the bush is so drab and nondescript for the rest of the year, and so glorious when you are gathering it down an English lane.

At the back of the shrubbery—or in the centre if it is an island site—you will need small trees. No forest giants here please. I advise the cherries (*Prunus*), the Crab-apples (*Malus*), *Amelanchier* (or poetically the Snowy Mespilus), the maples (*Acers*), some willows (*Salix*), the Robinias (False Acacias), and the willow-leaved pear (*Pyrus salicifolia* 'Pendula'); if you have a small garden and yearn avidly for a weeping willow and you can't have one because it will either undermine your foundations or make your garden as dry as dust because of all the water it needs, or block out every vestige of light—then the willow-leaved pear is your substitute, and not only that, its leaves are silver grey and its blossom purest white. Others to consider are hawthorn pink and white, laburnum, eucalyptus, black mulberry (*Morus nigra*), and sumach (*Rhus cotinus*). Do not overdo the planting of trees or in a few years' time you will have created too much shade, particularly for your sun-loving shrubs.

Aim always at informality. A tall tree here—there a short one—a deciduous pair and then a conifer. Conifers will have a later chapter all to themselves but I shall need to mention one or two here and cannot avoid repetition: columnar conifers like *Chamaecyparis lawsoniana* 'Columnaris' (blue) or *Cupressus macrocarpa* 'Goldcrest' (gold), or a proper fastigiate making a very narrow column, like *Juniperus communis* 'Hibernica' all provide very good exclamation marks amongst the modestly-sized shrubs—and both in the summer dusk and the poor light of winter, give the whole silhouette of the border an interesting shape. Group your colours artistically: copper beech next to *Cedrus atlantica*

'Glauca', silver weeping pear near copper maples or berberis, dark greens of solid conifer or yew providing the background for a silver maple. The golden leaves of the *Philadelphus coronarius* 'Aureus' are a wonderful foil for *Berberis thunbergii* 'Atropurpurea,' and next to the berberis on the other side put the bright blue grey of *Juniperus squamata* 'Meyeri'—three different colours and three different textures, with two of them deciduous with the evergreen conifer. There are so many combinations of foliage colour and texture that I must leave you to originate, experiment and copy some of the best examples which please your roving eye. As I write I look out on to a ceanothus which climbs a grey-brown stone wall; it has vigorously thrown its powder blue blooms atop of the enormous grey-pink and rose-mauve of a mop-head hydrangea (it could be *Hydrangea hortensia* 'Hamburg'); next to this is a large clump of *Anaphalis yedoensis*—the tallest variety with its white flowers and grey leaves. I didn't consciously strive for this very beautiful arrangement but when you get one like this, keep it.

Near the front of your shrub border, and indeed spreading over the ground of the border throughout it, in order to save labour, you will need ground cover. Heathers—many of which are sub-shrubs—are admirable (dealt with separately later). The spreading, prostrate conifers are excellent—*Juniperus communis* 'Repanda', *Juniperus procumbens* 'Nana', *Juniperus horizontalis* 'Glauca', *Taxus baccata* 'Repandens', which is a low growing and widely spreading yew. It does not mind dry shade, so is very valuable in a shrubbery. *Cistus*—not to be trusted in a hard winter, none of them are—*obtusifolius* is a small prostrate variety with smallish white flowers. Also evergreen is *Cotoneaster conspicuus* 'Decorus'—white flowers with red fruits, low-growing and excellent for covering banks. *C. horizontalis* is not evergreen—it is fan shaped or herringbone patterned with rich red leaves and fruit in the autumn. And evergreen again is *C. microphyllus* which has established itself at the bottom of some steps which lead to my courtyard—I am letting it cover as much as it likes to see how far it will go. As the courtyard is concrete covered with tar and gravel chips and is about 50 yards by 20 yards it will be interesting! The bees love it.

All the ivies (*Hedera*) are useful—remember the variegated ones become rather dark in the shade. The hebes or veronicas are all evergreen. *H. albicans* is hardy. *H. subalpina* needs sun and has white flowers.

Hypericum—the 'Rose of Sharon'—is a very vigorous ground coverer and will, if allowed, smother everything, you included;

its yellow flower with its feathery centre is one of the most beautiful in the garden.

Euonymus radicans 'Variegatus' is a trailing fan with grey-green leaves. Also *E. fortunei* 'Coloratus', evergreen, trailing and good for shade. *Cytisus procumbens* is a dwarf broom with prostrate branches but, like most brooms, it will need the sun. For continuous flowering, *Potentilla fruticosa* 'Longacre' is a dense mat with sulphur-yellow flowers. With greyish foliage, low spreading with white flowers, there also is *P. fruticosa* 'Mandshurica'. The creeping willow *Salix repens* 'Reticulata' needs a moist spot. Also there is *S. repens* 'Argentea' with silver-silky leaves. The evergreen Periwinkle will form extensive carpets of leaves and flowers in shade or sun. There are *Vinca major* with dark foliage and bright blue flowers, *V. major* 'Variegata', a creamy white form and *V. minor* 'Alba', a smaller periwinkle with white flowers. *V. minor* 'Atropurpurea' gives plum-coloured flowers. *Viburnum davidii* is evergreen and needs to be planted in groups of three or four so that they will cross-pollinate and give berries—if you want berries.

Whereas many of the above plants are for use between and under larger shrubs as ground cover, e.g. periwinkles and *Hypericum* 'Rose of Sharon'—the evergreen azalea needs to be featured in the front or the end or as a low bay or inlet into the shrubbery. Several need to be together for best effect and as their colours are very bright and striking you need to see them flowering in a garden centre before you decide on which will make the most effective neighbours. Try some of these for ground covering effect:— 'Arendsii', 'Dauntless', 'Koningin Wilhelmina', 'Leo' and 'Silver Moon', the latter being spreading but not so dwarf.

Santolina—various varieties of cotton lavender—make excellent ground cover. Lavandula 'Hidcote' and Lavandula 'Munstead' and *L. nana* 'Alba' (a white dwarf form) when planted close together also will do for ground cover, but surely we must save all lavenders for dwarf formal hedges and not waste them here.

By using some roses as ground cover, the most spectacular effects can be obtained from their flowers and their foliage. You would have to have plenty of room and they need very careful positioning, but here is an effect for you to try which is not much used in amateur gardens. I'm all for making the neighbours livid! *Rosa macrantha* is the rose to clothe your banks and annoy the neighbours with. Even the blooms are about 6 in. across, fragrant, pink which wears off to almost white. *Rosa hugonis,* if pruned in the right way, can be used almost as ground cover—its foliage is fern-like. Knowing not too much about it, I planted mine firstly to grow up a pergola pillar. This it refused to do because its nature really is to flop and spread—in quite early May it is covered with primrose-like and primrose yellow flowers—one of the earliest and daintiest of roses and so pleasant to look at for the rest of the summer—it's like a miniature robinia shrub in its foliage.

I do feel we must at last look to the shrubs which will form the larger part of our shrubbery. The best way to write about them is to suggest to you month-by-month the flowering shrubs and we will try and stick to as many fragrant ones as possible, and then we will make a list of foliage shrubs, indicating as we go their months of magnificence.

JANUARY is a month I don't really cater for. I am then in Pantomime so I cannot look round my garden unless I'm the Dame in *Jack and The Bean Stalk*! I think that gallant though some flowers are—and springlike though some Januarys may be—even when an exquisite flower is produced, a wind, a winter shower or a heavy frost will make it look sad and out of place. However, some gardeners (Beverley Nichols is one of them) greatly favour the trumpetings of the first flowers and look forward to them as the true spring harbingers they are. Here again, it helps if you are in the south, west, or sheltered midlands—or have a whiff of the Gulf Stream in the west of Scotland. There is a fragrant Camellia which comes out in January—it must be sheltered by a wall, and has small white flowers—*C. sasanqua.* Did you know, by the way, that when you go and buy a quarter of a pound of tea to drink you are buying camellia leaves? *C. sinensis,* natives of China and India.

The Winter Sweet is so aptly named; its flowers are small and not very beautiful with waxy yellow flowers with a browny-purple centre on leafless branches, but be warned, it does not flower for several years. It lasts about three weeks in water. I find it difficult to describe the scent of anything for, as with colour, everyone's appreciation of fragrance varies, but I'd say Winter Sweet has a kind of vanilla scent. Don't prune it—only what you take in for the house to enliven the dark days.

If you like oddities, then *Garrya elliptica* will please you. It's a very dark-leaved evergreen shrub—not too hardy, especially in its first few years with you. Make sure you get the male plant. If you do, it will have greyish-green pendulous catkins which hang in clusters. There is a variety with extra long catkins called 'James Roof'. There is a summer flowering variety, but it is in January that it is so valuable.

The witch hazel—*Hamamelis*—is so fragile with its whorling yellow flowers that you think it cannot possibly last a moment —but it really contradicts my earlier remarks about shabby winter flowers. It stays immaculate. It grows very slowly so don't cut too much of it each winter until you have a large shrub. There is a variety *H. intermedia* 'Diane' which is red, and 'Magic Fire', orangy-red. *Hamamelis mollis* is the Chinese witch hazel and the commonest one. I am sure there is a variety which has extravagantly contorted branches but I cannot find its name, no matter how I search. Perhaps I have imagined it!

Of the heathers, *Erica carnea* do in fact start in November, but they are wonderful pushing up gallantly through the snow— particularly 'Springwood White'; it's literally as white as snow. There is also 'Springwood Pink' and 'King George', a brighter pink. 'Eileen Porter' has rich dark and low growing flowers.

Jasminum nudiflorum is strictly a climber and does well against a north wall—its bright yellow little flowers are most welcome in January. Vita Sackville-West suggested once, I believe, that it should be planted to grow in loose masses from a 6 ft. high support such as rambler roses have, on those rose standard crinoline frames. I've never seen it grown this way but I should think it would be fabulous. I'm putting one to grow up my dove-cote this autumn. It is good for terrace walls, both to grow up them and down them from the top; it's so self-rooting that you will always be giving it away. *Lonicera fragrantissima* is not a climbing honeysuckle as such, it is a shrub with fragrant cream flowers.

No January garden will be complete without *Viburnum tinus* 'Laurustinus'. It will have started most generously to flower in December in a sheltered spot—it has glossy dark leaves with a reddish underside. Its flowers are flat and white, shaped like the wild yarrow—pink when in bud—and it goes on and on and on flowering—even in the shade. It takes a little while to grow at first. When you get your plant from the nurserymen you think it is very small indeed. It will remain so for the first two years and then suddenly it's away and can become a large shrub. No shrubbery is complete without one of these. There is also *Viburnum bodnantense* which begins in October and flowers the winter through. This is fragrant.

F E B R U A R Y begins the exciting time with lots of little bulbs flowering and the promise of spring. According to the season all the foregoing shrubs suggested for January may not commence until February—similarly most of them will be in flower with the following suggestions: *Daphne mezereum* is a must, but it prefers chalk soils. It's a little difficult in my acid bit of Sussex, but I will never forget it blooming on a cold wet February morning in Kings Heath Park, Birmingham, where we assembled for my TV Gardening programme. It has a honeyed scent and it seemed so incongruous on that dark morning. It will grow 5 ft. high— has dark wine-coloured blooms—but there is also a white one, *D. m.* 'Alba'. The berries are very poisonous—red for *D. mezereum* and yellow for *D. m.* 'Alba'. They will also grow from seed sown in July.

There is an additional honeysuckle for February called *Lonicera setifera,* which looks like the Daphne, and *Lonicera standishii* with exceptionally sweetly-scented cream flowers.

Dogwood—*Cornus alba* 'Sibirica'—is red and looks wonderful against the snow. It is the red stems we are looking for—not flowers. You prune it hard in March. There is also *C. stolonifera* 'Flaviramea' which is yellow and a good contrast. Remember, though, the dogwoods need a damp spot. *Cornus mas* 'Variegata' is the Cornelian Cherry—a small tree or large shrub with small yellow flowers in February. It is in the camellia corner at Hidcote—the famous garden in Gloucestershire.

Mahonia aquifolium: this means 'with leaves shaped like holly'; they are broad and prickly with, after its bright yellow flowers produced in crowded sprays, violet black berries, which accounts for its other name of Oregon Grape. There is also *M. a.* 'Atropurpurea', where the leaves are a chestnut purple in the winter and spring. This plant is often used in woodland for coverts—it does not mind shade—and can be bought fairly cheaply in quantity but only if you have a very large garden. I have *M. a.* 'Bealei'. It is very heavily scented with shorter and more upright flowers.

Rhododendron dauricum has bright rose-purple flowers in February. So has *R. yunnanense* 'Praecox'. By the way, 'praecox' means early. *R. mucronulatum* flowers from December to February according to the season and again it is rose-purple.

Common Gorse—*Ulex europaeus*—flowers almost the whole year through but quite often it obliges most beautifully in February. It is self-seeding and you will be plagued with tiny spiny seedlings; however, the bother of fetching your gloves to weed these is worth it, for the heady fruity scent of the blooms. Put it on the driest, stoniest, poorest bit of sunny soil you have in the garden. It revels in poverty.

MARCH has a great richness of flowering shrubs. *Camellia*

iaponica should be grown where the early morning sun cannot de-frost them too quickly as this 'burns' them and the flowers are then tinged with brown and spoilt. Place them to face the west and never the east. There are so many varieties and most of them are perfectly hardy. It is best in the south to give them some kind of shade—not too much—and in the north to let them have more sun to harden the young growth. There are several thousand named varieties and I do not intend to mention many. There are the *C. williamsii* hybrids which are perhaps the best for shrubberies, free flowering from the New Year to May. *C. w.* 'Donation' is large, pink, semi-double but with prominent golden anthers; the leaves are more pointed than most, which are usually laurel shaped. *C. w.* 'Coppelia Alba' is white and single, and 'Caerhays' is lilac-rose. Remember they are woodland plants and need a peaty soil. There are several forms of flowers, i.e. single, semi-double, anemone form, Paeony form, rose form and the genuine double form which rarely show their stamens or anthers.

Magnolias need a sheltered site free from the wind and spring frost and many of them become, with good soil and plenty of rich manuring and humus, quite large trees, although the majority are slow-growing. One sees many a splendid specimen growing in the front garden of some seedy suburban villa, having grown in beauty as the house and district have declined, which is evidence of the fact that magnolias are most tolerant of atmospheric pollution. Don't be too put off by the catalogues and text books which tell you that magnolias will not flower for many years. I have three which gave me many blooms in their second year. *Magnolia denudata* (which is best when in flower in April for it misses the frost and wind then) grows fairly quickly and blooms when young. Position it like a camellia for the same reason—no early sun. *Magnolia campbellii* opens its flowers in February sometimes, and continues in March. It is a large spectacular creature, white or pink with several named varieties, some of these fragrant. There is also *Magnolia stellata*, a small shrub—somewhat un-magnolia-like, almost strap-like petals. Don't put it where it's windy as the flowers will suffer terribly. It grows slowly but flowers when quite young.

The Japanese Quince—Cydonia I call it but we have to learn to call it *Chaenomeles* now. It is best on a wall but makes a small shrub for the front of the border. It has orange and red flowers with yellow stamens. There is a white one *C. lagenaria* 'Snow'. You can make quince jelly with the fruit, but I'd rather use the real quince. Some say it is the forbidden fruit of the Bible—in which case Adam's teeth were magnificent. It is bullet-hard!

Forsythia we all know for its prolific star-like flowers of canary yellow. You should prune it after flowering and never in the autumn, otherwise you will not get any flowers the following spring. Similarly finches, in some areas, denude the shrub of buds and you don't get flowers then. There is a weeping variety used to cover walls but the flowers are not so prolific as *F. spectabilis*—but if you have a very small garden I'd get *F. ovata* which is dwarf, scented and perhaps earlier than March.

Prunus cerasifera 'Pissardii Nigra' is a purple-foliaged flowering plum. The flowers are soft pink. I have one where the flowers are a deep pink, almost red, and with the purple foliage it is most beautiful. It is a tree, but it can be a large shrub if you let its suckers (which come from its trunk sometimes) take over—I have done this in a shrubbery and it is now an enormously beautiful shrub but I don't suppose I should have allowed this to happen.

Rhododendron racemosum—with bright pink flowers and with leaves whose undersides are glaucous—flowers in March, but then in an early season so do a lot of the April-flowering ones. *R. racemosum* is lime-tolerant! Or perhaps it would be best to say—it can cope with a certain degree of alkalinity. *R. hirsutum* is another. *R. moupinese* is a dwarf evergreen shrub with purple-spotted white flowers in March. *R. lutescens* carries her lemon yellow flowers in March and she grows to 4 ft. *R. fulgens* is a brilliant crimson and a really old bush (I had one at my last house). It will grow to 15 ft. high. It has chestnut red bark and the underside of its leaves are the same colour. This one is often earlier than March, but again it depends on its position, locality and the mildness of the winter. If you want a white one for March, try *R. cyclium*—the flowers are scented.

APRIL is so bountiful: there is such a burgeoning of blossom at this season that it is difficult to choose from so much magnificence. There are some glorious foliage shrubs in April, principally the Acers. *Acer negundo fraxinifolia* 'Alba Variegata' is a tree with variegated leaves of green and white, and contrasts effectively with *A. platanoides* —the Norway Maple— 'Crimson King' which has large leaves of deep crimson purple. Amelanchiers I have mentioned.

Let us consider the berberis. Many flower in May but *Berberis darwinii* flowers in April. They are a striking orange-yellow and hang in clusters. The leaves are evergreen and like tiny dark green shiny holly leaves. It has small bluish berries in the autumn. *Berberis stenophylla* is beautiful with its graceful pendulous branches and its gloriously scented yellow flowers. It is most useful for hedges for it is spiny, grows quickly and is densely entwined with itself. *B. hookeri* has green spiny leaves and branches with pale yellow flowers. *Berberis thunbergii* 'Atropurpurea' is reddish-purple and chestnut and is such a gracefully shaped shrub. Place it next to a blue juniper and you have a breathtaking combination of colours.

Camellias come in April, too; so do many of the Chaenomeles.

Cytisus—the brooms, are prominent now and add their blooms and fragrance to the scene. Many of these can be grown quickly from seed and are well worth sowing for they are short lived and make excellent filling-in material to help establish a new shrubbery, and to dispense with later when the slower growing and more permanent shrubs take their place. You should prune back the plant as soon as the flowers fade, but do not savagely prune at all or the shrubs will die. They need a lot of sun. *C. beanii* is about a foot in height with small golden-yellow flowers. *C. praecox* stays compact without pruning and has primrose-yellow flowers. *C. albus* is white and flowers in May as well. *C. purgans* is yellow and fragrant.

Several of the Daphnes flower in April but I don't know very much about them, I'm afraid.

The tree heather flowers in April.

Kerria japonica is often grown against walls but it also looks well in a shrubbery. It has bright yellow flowers and *K. japonica* 'Pleniflora' is double and flowers for a longer period. It suckers easily so you will always have plenty to give away.

Amongst the April magnolias is *M. soulangiana* which flowers on bare branches with white tulip-shaped flowers with soft purple at the base. *M. s.* 'Alba Superba' is white and scented. *M. denudata* is a large shrub with white goblet-shaped flowers. *M. soulangiana* 'Lennei' has flowers of rose-purple and settles in very quickly (mine flowered the first spring).

Malus—the crab-apple—is an effective shrub as well as a tree. *M. lemionei* is purple-leaved with red flowers and small fruit rather like a dullish cherry in the autumn. *M. floribunda* is the Japanese Crab with crimson buds opening to white. *Malus robusta* is the Siberian Crab. I had two in my first garden at Old Welwyn in Hertfordshire—the flowers are white and the fruit on one tree, 'Red Siberian', was bright red, and bright yellow on the Siberian Yellow; they were not standards, they were shrubs and so generous with colour at both ends of the season. *M. sargentii* is also more of a shrub than a tree, with white flowers and cherry-like fruits.

Osmanthus, I must mention, though I have never owned one. The flowers of *O. delavayi* are white and fragrant and jasmine-like.

Pieris I do know and what a great acquaintance! But only on acid soil I fear. The flowers are in clusters, a little like lily-of-the-valley and with the same strong compelling fragrance. *P. forrestii* 'Wakehurst' is perhaps the best. The bonus with this shrub is the brilliantly red bracts—rather like a Poinsettia—which happen in spring. Then there is *P. japonica* 'Variegata' with silvery, creamy-white leaves flushed with pink—but, oh, it does grow slowly, but this may be because I have placed it badly in too dry a spot.

The flowering currant looks spectacular but smells rather of cats! Particularly if you pick it and bring it into the house. Prune it hard for the first five years. There are about twenty species but I can recommend *Ribes sanguineum* 'Pulborough Scarlet' and *R. s.* 'Album', white. *R. s.* 'Splendens' has larger flowers of rosy-crimson.

Frederick Street, in his authoritative book on *Rhododendrons* (Cassell & Co.) says it is too dangerous a method to name different weeks or months in which they flower and most wisely suggests very early-Christmas-time to mid-April; early-April; Early mid-season—mid-April to mid-May; Mid-season—May; Late mid-May to mid-June; and very late mid-June. There is also the *Rhododendron Handbook* of the Royal Horticultural Society which deals with the whole subject, species and hybrids from A–Z. 'Ah! 'you are saying, 'Here is Fletcher sliding out of giving his recommendations to us and I have waded this far for this very information'. But from April to June there are literally hundreds of kinds, together with the evergreen azaleas to choose from. And they vary from R. *falconeri* which grows up to 50 ft. high, to R. *fastigiatum,* a close-growing cushion-shaped mat! I will mention a few of the hardiest, taken at random here and there, but do go to the Chelsea Show, go to some of the great gardens and go to your garden centre and meet the plants in person. Rhododendrons, being surface rooted, are admirable plants for containers and 'instant gardening'.

R. *campanulatum* is very hardy with white or lavender bell-shaped flowers spotted with purple, about 8 ft. high. There is a

'Knaphill' variety which is nearly blue. R. *canadense* is a deciduous dwarf azalea—pink flowers with grey-felted green leaves, 3 ft. high and very hardy. R. *chryseum* 'Lapponicum' is a dwarf evergreen shrub with yellow flowers, 1 ft. high. R. *dauricum* is semi-evergreen, medium sized, 1–2 ft. and with white rose-purple flowers. R. *hippophaeoides* has small grey-green aromatic leaves; of 3–4 ft. in height with blue flowers. R. *microleucum* is a pure white dwarf rhododendron of great merit, suitable for the rock garden so it must be very much in front. R. *thomsonii* is a small tree with red bark, blood-red bell-shaped flowers with darker base. It has dark leaves which are white-grey beneath and grows to 12 ft. high. (Not quite so hardy as my other recommendations.) R. *yunnanense,* free growing, floriferous pinky-white flowers with dark red spots—grows up to 5 ft. high.

Now for a selection of hybrids which flower in April. I wanted speed when I chose the thirty-three rhododendrons shrubs I planted in my garden here—ranging from April to June for blooming. They flower at the right time but now, after six years, they are large leggy things and I wish I had been patient. Have some quick ones for the back of your border and the extremity of your wood by all means but *vary* the kinds and shapes and habit always in everything to do with a garden.

'Ascot Brilliant' is bright crimson but needs a bit of shade. 'Bibiani' is rich dark crimson and is tall growing. A dwarf dark crimson is 'Carmen'. Red with a striking dark blotch is 'Chevalier Felix de Sauvage'. 'Early Brilliant' is scarlet. 'Cinnkeys' is orange-yellow with bell-like flowers. 'Crossbill' is moderate in height—needs a bit of shelter—yellow tinted with brick red, perhaps apricot—well buy one and see!

'Devonshire Cream' is creamy-yellow with a red blotch at the base to be the fruit with the cream tea. Semi-deciduous because it is an azaleadendron. 'Glory of Littleworth', pale yellow with an orange eye. 'Goldfort', creamy-yellow tinged with apricot, was one of the best new rhododendrons of 1962. 'Goldsworth Yellow' is another in this colour range. 'Goldsworth Pink' is deep rose fading to white. Bright rose-pink that will grow anywhere is 'Jacksonii'. A smallish shrub with blush pink flowers is 'Racil'. 'Susan' is tall with near blue flowers. And for white, 'Handsworth Early White' is very hardy. 'Dame Nellie Melba' is vigorous and has large flesh pink flowers fading to blush.

Moving on from the rhododendrons, spiraea is a good medium-sized shrub. It is wreathed in white flowers in April.

Viburnum burkwoodii has fragrant white flowers, try the clone 'Fulbrook'. *V. carlessi* has downy leaves, green above, greyish beneath, needs good soil and is richly fragrant.

Thus the flowers of April pass as quickly as they always do. There is so much activity in the garden at this time and so much to do and see that one rushes, almost without noticing, headlong into the riot of colour and fragrance that is May.

MAY. The Japanese maples or acers are first because they come so alphabetically, but they are first, too, because of their beauty, even though they do not flower. They must have an acid soil and they prefer shelter. As the buds unfold, the leaves are very tender green and there is a soft downiness about them like a beech bud unfolding. *A. palmatum* 'Atropurpureum' is deep crimson. Its tender ruby foliage, with the spring sun through it, is most beautiful and in the autumn comes magnificence again. *Acer palmatum* has bright yellow-green foliage to start with and *A. dissectum* 'Atropurpureum' has finely cut purple leaves.

Many camellias wait till May if you have the later variety, and you are sure of a perfect flower, though I think the May of 1946 had snow which broke my pink Japanese cherry trees with the weight of it on the blossom. The pink and white flowers through the snow were a glorious sight, and we had vast trees in that garden.

Ceanothus is the best blue-flowered shrub to be grown in this country. It comes from California and is known as the Californian lilac. Its blooms are the same shape as lilac but much smaller, about 2 in. long. Ceanothus need good drainage and are lime tolerant. Are they evergreen? Well, it depends a little where you live and how sheltered the position. Prune—if you have to—immediately after flowering. Mine never seem to stop flowering. They start in the spring, they have another go in August and seem to carry on until the first frosts. This may account for the fact that they are short-lived sometimes and might collapse after a hard winter. *C.* 'Cascade' is evergreen, spring flowering and bright blue. *C. rigidus* is violet blue and of the deciduous hybrids, 'Marie Simon' is pink—but there are so many pink shrubs let's give her the cold shoulder and have 'Southmead' who is bright blue in May and evergreen again.

Ought I to call azaleas 'rhododendrons' or 'azaleas'? Let's talk about a few as azaleas so that not all of us are confused. There are Japanese azaleas, which are various forms of *Rhododendron obtusum*, tall or dwarf in a vast range of colour. The 'Kurume' azaleas, which are all forms of *R. obtusum*, are evergreen. Here are a few: 'Amoenum'—magenta; 'Apple Blossom' —no need to describe; 'Hi-No-Degeri'—bright crimson; 'Hi-No-Mayo' is a soft pink; 'Kure-No-Yuki' is pure white, and 'Toreoda' is bright red.

Then come the hybrid Japanese azaleas. These have larger flowers than the Karumes. 'Blue Danube ' is blue-purple; 'Blaauw's Pink' is a bright cerise; 'Favourite', a deep rosy-pink; 'John Cairns' is orange-red and flowers best in partial shade. 'Malvaticum' is mauve; 'Aladdin' pillar box red, or the red of Chinese lacquer or Widow Twankey's nose! 'Palestrina' is the only white I know and it is tallish with large flowers tinged with green.

We all know the sweetly scented common *Azalea ponticum* with yellow flowers and the brightest red autumn leaves. A group of these will scent a woodland glade.

There are also the famous Knaphill azaleas which are deciduous hybrids. They grow up to 8 ft. in height and they range from creamy-white through yellow and orange and apricot to orange-scarlet, tangerine, vermillion to dark red. There is even a brownish-orange one called 'Ginger'. And one called 'Homebush' is violet pink.

Azalea mollis give a rich display of colour in May and are deciduous. Those of you who have been to the Savill Gardens at Windsor in May will have been dazzled by the display of azaleas. Many of these are the Windsor hybrids. The 'Ghent' azaleas are hybrids from *Azalea ponticum*—they are hardy and have small later flowers.

Smelling of hawthorn are the white flowers of the Mexican Orange Tree—*Choisya ternata*. It needs a sunny corner for the wood to ripen thoroughly for the coming winter's frosts and it will grow to 8 ft. or so. It is a rounded evergreen bush.

The Cistus is a rock rose and largely a Mediterranean family, so you will need to take cuttings each year for fear of losing some. For the same reason have it on a sunny, well-drained sheltered part of the shrubbery. I love them, not only for the flower but for the fragrance of the plant itself, especially *C. ladaniferus* which grows to 5 ft., has large crinkly white flowers, sometimes with blotches of maroon at the base as you look inside the flower. *C. cyprius* has a blood-red patch. *C. albidus* has leaves covered with feltish down—pale lilac-pink flowers which are single-rose-like. *C. purpureus* has what I call 'shocking pink' flowers. *C.* 'Silver Pink' is a very hardy hybrid produced by Messrs Hilliers. These shrubs have an atmosphere of old gardens about them, difficult for me to describe. They settle in well and grow quickly (and die quickly, too, I'm afraid). They help a garden to look mature—I'm mad about them.

Do not confuse the Cistus with Cytisus which are brooms. *C. kewensis* is a trailing variety for May, *C. purpureus* flowers with pale purple pea flowers from May to July. Often in May, but mostly in June, comes a broom of great distinction and difference, *C. battandieri,* which comes from Morocco. It is tall—mine is 12 ft. high by a wall and balustrade—and has large, greyish, clover-like leaves on a leggy plant (perhaps this is my fault), whose white downy stems terminate in golden-yellow, cone-shaped flowers about 2 in. long, and are composed of tightly-packed vetch-like flowers which smell strongly and delightfully of pineapple. It has got a touch of the laburnum about it with its trefoil leaves. Laburnum is a riot of blossom in May. *L. anagyroides* is the common variety and I have always intended to have an avenue of them with standard wistarias as alternate trees—do visualise this for a moment. I'll have it one day. *Wistaria floribunda* has violet-blue slender flowers which are fragrant. There is *W. alba,* white tinted with violet. And for very long racemes indeed there is *W. macrobotrys*. The popular one is *W. sinensis,* the Chinese Wisteria.

Whilst talking of climbers, Clematis comes in May.

Daphne burkwoodii has very fragrant pale pink flowers in clusters in May, and *D. caucasica* has white flowers in May and June. *D. alpina* is tiny and suitable for the rockery. It has white flowers and orange-red fruits. *D. collina* is also only a foot high and has scented lilac flowers.

Enkianthus campanulatus has bell-shaped flowers ranging in colour from cream to bronze. It grows to 9 ft. high and has a profusion of flowers, a bit like lily-of-the-valley, for at least three weeks. Its autumn foliage is magic. *E. palibinni* has red flowers.

Genista falcata is the Spanish Gorse. *G. lydia* is dwarf and spreading, likes the dry, and has yellow flowers.

There are many climbing honeysuckles (*Lonicera*) which flower in May but *L. hispida* is a hardy bristly-leaved shrub with pale yellow flowers. *L. syringantha* is a small shrub of rounded habit with sweetly-scented lilac flowers and small leaves.

Paeonies have exciting flowers for herbaceous plants—large and scented and beautiful, but when I tell you there is a tree paeony—actually a large shrub—then one's mind begins boggling. Full sun they need and a sheltered site and their roots don't mind any degree of frost—it is the early delicate shoots which need protection from the spring frosts. *Paeonia delavayi* flowers in May, deeply red with golden anthers. *P. lemoinei* is yellow. They all have large, dramatic flowers and deeply cut glamorous foliage. They need a rich soil.

The Olearia are from the Antipodes. They are tree daisies—evergreen, good for the sea-side, sun loving and good for chalky soils. The one which I remember best was on acid soil at Great Dixter—it must have been 15 ft. high and as much round. It was *O. macrodonta*—white, felty on the underside, holly-like leaves and the whole bush a magnificent sight covered with white daisies the size and shape of a Michaelmas daisy, only in clusters. Mr Lloyd assured me of its hardiness when completely grown, and although Great Dixter is in Sussex and it had a sheltered position by a low wall and near to a barn—it is *East* Sussex and we do not have the warm zephyrs of the Gulf Stream. It was richly scented and even when not in bloom the plant like the Cistus adds an aroma all its own to the garden. So do *Cupressus lawsoniana* in the sun and many of the Eucalyptus. It is these aromas which give a garden its maturity and, to me, many of its joys. There is an *Olearia odorata* which is especially fragrant in July.

Potentillas are forever in flower May to September. This is its remarkable attraction for all gardeners. It is easy to grow; give it plenty of sunshine. There are harbaceous potentillas of similar generosity. *P. fruticosa* grows to about 4 ft. in height and is covered with bright yellow primrose-like flowers over a long period. There are many hybrid named varieties of the *P. fruticosa*, some with greyish foliage and orange flowers, all shades of yellow and pure white and creamy-white. You must have these in your garden and because they are always in flower, which must be so exhausting, in the winter they sham as if dead—but for goodness sake do not be fooled by this and throw such treasures away. Come May and June they will be as bright as any part of your garden. 'Sunset' and 'Tangerine' are two of the orange ones, and 'Tangerine' is quite partial to a lacy shade. 'Elizabeth' is very beautiful.

Pyracantha flowers profusely in May and the flowers are hawthorn-like, but it is the fruits of red, orange and yellow in the autumn with which the shrubs are covered that make them a must. Evergreen against a north wall, they are invaluable. *P.* 'Orange Glow' has orange fruits. *P.* 'Knap Hill Lemon' is a clone of *P. crenatoserrata*; the fruits are bright yellow. For red fruits choose *P. atalantioides*—they are scarlet and long lasting.

I would like to make a note here on some of the cherries

(*Prunus*) for May. Very useful indeed (with me this one does not suffer bird damage like the others—perhaps they are fooled by the shape!) is *P. amanogawa*—the Lombardy poplar cherry with large pale-pink semi-double flowers close to the tree. Did I mention *Prunus* 'Pandora' in April—Vita Sackville-West says *P.* 'Pandora' is virginal—'She emerges from her stem as a débutante from her first ball dress'.* *P.* 'Shidari-Sakura' weeps enchanting deep bright-pink blooms, and *P.* 'Ukon' (*serrulata grandiflora*) has large semi-double pale-yellow flowers tinged with green, and as these are flowering against the newly-minted bronzy-green foliage 'Ukon' is good to Lukon. Sorry!

Rhododendrons for May include amongst the species *R. aberconwayi*, small to medium, with pure white flowers which commence pink and are slightly spotted maroon. *R. caloxanthus* has citron-yellow flowers which are orange-red in bud, bell-shaped in clusters. It is hardy and comes from Tibet. 'Augustinii' needs woodland shade and the 'Chasmanthum' variety is a tall, quick-growing shrub with lavender flowers. *R. litiense* has soft yellow flowers and is a large shrub.

May-flowering Rhododendron hybrids include *R.* 'Adriaan Koster'—medium height and creamy-yellow; *R.* 'Alice Waterer'—tall with sugar-pink flowers. *R.* 'Bagshot Ruby'—cherry-red and is very hardy. *R.* 'Beauty of Littleworth' is a giant with white trusses spotted with dark crimson. *R.* 'Betty Wormald' has large trusses of coral-pink flowers spotted on the upper petals. *R.* 'Black Beauty' is deep maroon of medium height (mine this summer and for no understandable reason, has died). *R.* 'Constant Nymph' is of medium height with white flowers. *R.* 'Countess of Athlone' is tall, quick-growing, semi-double and the most beautiful light mauve—fairy-like on a May evening. *R.* 'Cynthia' is rosy-crimson. *R.* 'David' is blood-red. *R.* 'Elspeth' is of medium height and is salmon fading to cream. *R.* 'Fastuosum is very hardy, tall and double mauve with a green eye. *R.* 'Firebird'—brilliant orange-scarlet. And a new one, *R.* 'Golden Fleece', is medium height with golden-yellow frilled flowers. *R.* 'Honey' is tall and yellow. *R.* 'Langworth' is vigorous growing with large white flowers and chocolate throat. I will conclude the hybrid rhododendrons with perhaps the most famous one of all, *R.* 'Pink Pearl'. It is tall-growing with large trusses of clear shell-pink flowers.

The species roses begin to flower in April—that is to say some of them—and go on into June, so I will introduce a selection to you here. They grow everywhere, being very

* *V. Sackville-West's Garden Book.* Published by Michael Joseph.

hardy as to climate. They prefer sun and they do not like a very acid soil. Otherwise they are pretty trouble-free and do not need pruning either, except for the odd thinning out now and then and the removal of dead branches. Many of them repeat flowering if you remove the dead heads of the first crop, and many of them have most decorative hips. Many are good for hedging and some of them are seen best on their own standing in grass—when their graceful form is given free rein and we can see a vast mound of blossom. Hilliers' Nursery at Winchester has many of them displayed in this way, whereas the late Vita Sackville-West had them in beds with low box edging which gives the most marvellous period effect. At Hidcote they form natural members of great mixed borders, and Mr Lloyd at Great Dixter does both. I have only just come to realise their charm, and for us busy amateur gardeners how easy they are to look after. Many of them are climbing species for walls, pergolas and trellis.

> 'I saw the sweetest flower wild nature yields.
> A fresh blown musk-rose 'twas the first that threw
> Its sweets upon the summer; graceful it grew
> As is the wand that Queen Titania wields
> And as I feasted on its fragrancy,
> I thought the garden rose it much excelled.'
>
> Keats

There are well over two hundred species roses and many hybrids of them, and many new/old roses are being evolved if you will pardon an Irishism. The great authority on old roses, and one who has done so much to make them popular, is Mr Graham Thomas, and if you need to know more than I can tell you in my rough hotch-potch way, then you should get his book *The Old Shrub Roses*, or the late Mr Edward Bunyard's book *Old Garden Roses*; he is another authority.

Species roses have the most wonderfully poetic names: Musk roses, Bourbon roses, Damask roses and China roses. It was the last two who gave birth, in the early nineteenth century, to the Bourbon roses. Then there are the Cabbage roses, Moss roses, Centifolias and Gallicas. My wife, Betty Astell, has for some years been an enthusiastic needleworker—making carpets, fire-screens in Petit-point, footstools, bell-pulls—you may have seen some of her lovely work on television. Well, it is in the old Dutch paintings and embroideries where one sees these old roses in profusion and to perfection. Centifolia, the cabbage rose, is known also as 'Rose de Peintures' because of its association with the old Dutch painters.

We will commence with the White Rose of York—R. *alba*. It is certainly old enough for the legend of this rose being the Yorkist emblem in the Wars of the Roses, and some say that the Romans knew of it. It is a partial damask! Beware, for some *albas* are pink, e.g. R. *alba* 'Maiden's Blush', and this was known as far back as 1697.

R. *gallica* 'Officinalis' is the Red Rose of Lancaster. It is sometimes known as the Old Red Damask, which sounds a little like a Cardinal who has been at the port! Some think *Rosa mundi*—the white and red striped rose—was the one which brought the factions together—but others that it was R. *damascena* 'Versicolor'.

R. *foetida* is the 'Austrian Yellow'. There is also the 'Austrian Copper', which I prefer; it is coppery-red with a yellow reverse, R. 'Bicolor'. R. 'Marigold', a newer rose, is by far the best coppery climber I know; its scent is glorious; its shape is most graceful and it flowers twice a season with large semi-double open flowers.

R. 'Highdownensis' is a medium-sized shrub with large velvety crimson single flowers but it also has the most spectacular flagon-shaped hips. This is at Hidcote and it so impressed me I wrote it down and got one. I was not disappointed. This is a seedling of *Rosa moyesii*, whose flowers are blood-red and crimson.

The Banksian rose is fragrant, early and a climber. Its flowers are white and smell of violets. If it is cold it won't flower—a warm sheltered corner, please, with plenty of sun to ripen the new wood. R. *b.* 'Lutea' is yellow and R. *b.* 'Normalis' is creamy white.

Rosa brunonii is a white climbing Musk rose. R. *b.* 'La Mortola' is the best form. R. 'Canary Bird' I have already told you about. R. *cantabrigiensis* has fragrant leaves—so, of course, has the Sweet Briar with pure pink flowers and bright red fruit. They are supposed to flower all the summer—mine hardly flower at all and I have many in various positions dotted about the garden. I bought a job-lot of a dozen cheaply. It never does in the long run—always go to the reputable dealer and buy the best. There are also the Lord Penzance briars. 'Lady Penzance' has coppery-yellow flowers and 'Amy Robsart' is deep rose.

Have you read the sort of novel where the heroine is breathtakingly beautiful? I have got to use this phrase now. I have repeatedly advised that you should visit—as an artist would make frequent sorties to the National Gallery or the Tate or the Louvre—some of the great gardens; no matter where you live there must be one quite near. I went to Sissinghurst Castle three years ago in June—I turned the corner into the White Garden with my wife—we were speechless—it was breathtakingly beautiful—the whole poetic confection of white and grey and green was very lovely, but in the centre of this garden (and later we saw great mountains of them garlanding the trees in the orchard) was R. *filipes* 'Kiftsgate' at its perfect best. It is an extremely vigorous rose and will clothe a tree in two or three years—its flowers are fragrant and about the size of the old half-crown, borne in enormous panicles of perhaps twenty flowers a time—all sweetly scented and so very white. We saw a huge mound of fragrant clusters of white flowers against a blue sky and trailing to the ground. It needs space. It is a positive pageant of a plant. Go out and get one at once; you will never look a hybrid tea in the face again!

Have I properly described a Moss rose ? R. *centifolia* 'Muscosa' has a dense moss-like covering of bristles which overlay the buds, the calyx, the stems and branches. The moss is usually darker than the rest of the leaves and stems, and to the touch it is stickily resinous—the flowers are pink, heavily globular and richly scented. R. *m.* 'Cristata' is double, deep pink, with very dark mossing. R. *m.* 'Golden Moss' has peach-yellow flowers and R. *m.* 'Gloire de Mousseuses' has large double pink flowers and greyish foliage, slightly subject to mildew. R. *m.* 'Nuits de Young' is also called the Old Black Moss. It has velvety maroon-purple petals in double blooms, a dark moss and the yellow stamens make the flowers seem darker still. R. *m.* 'Oeillet Panachee' has double white flowers striped with red and is hardy. 'William Lobb' has double flowers of carmine shaded with violet which fade to a greyish lavender. I wonder if Barrie named his gnome-like character in *Dear Brutus* after him ?* In the red border at Hidcote I noted down R. 'Rosemary Rose' but I don't seem to be able to find any catalogue mentioning her. A vermillion-scarlet, as I recall, and very, very red. Perhaps she's a floribunda or a hybrid tea who has slipped in here by mistake.

One of the beauties of the old roses is the amount of blueness in their pinks; they are almost a silvery-pink with a mauve

* I am being fanciful. William Lobb was a famous plant collector in the middle of the nineteenth century and this rose was first introduced in 1855.

blueness about them. *R. woodsii* is one of these lilac-pinks and *Rosa rugosa* 'Roseraie de l'Hay' is a rich crimson bluish-purple—getting bluer as it fades—but with me I do not get a shrub covered in blooms as I feel I should—just two or three blooms continuously through the summer. In a gardening note-book I keep, I noted down a reference from Fred Whitsey (the Editor of *Popular Gardening*) of 'Tour de Malakoff', which is all shades of blue and purple through the life of the bloom, but I can find no reference to it anywhere else. 'Mermaid' is a lovely single yellow for a climbing rose—a really beautiful flower and very popular, but it is not vigorous and not very hardy, although it was recommended to me for a north wall.

And to finish this dissertation on the old and specie roses, what about a green rose? This is a *Rosa chinensis*—the China Rose. *R. c.* 'Viridiflora' is a small shrub with double flowers seemingly made up of serrated green leaves tinted with bronze—I would not want it even though it does flower, like the rest of the China roses, from June to October.

Let us remind ourselves that this is a chapter on shrubberies and all the shrub roses are perfect for inclusion in a shrubbery. So are several—indeed very many —of the floribunda roses. Not, however, the hybrid teas. You cannot mix so stylised a flower with other shrubs. On the other hand, the floribunda is acknowledged as the best 'bedding' flower. I shall recommend a few floribundas for general shrubbery use as I did with species roses for ground cover and we will have a separate chapter entitled 'The Rose Garden'.

If you need in your shrubbery a good solid block of white to flower for long periods, three or four Iceberg floribundas will do the job very nicely. You will have a fragrance—a very pretty flower opening fully to show its anthers as a semi-double—a very controllably-sized shrub for the middle of the border. No staking required—just dead-head the flowers as you go along. '*Masquerade*' will supply a similar orange-cum-red-cum-yellow cum-blue effect, accordingly to the age of the bloom. Also for the back of a shrubbery, or the centre of an island site, to give you a profusion of blooms from June to October, the tall, vigorous 'Queen Elizabeth'. 'Elizabeth of Glamis' is not so tall but it is deep salmon with perfect shape and a stronger fragrance. 'Allgold' is also not so tall but has a yellow flower fading to primrose and good foliage. They are trying to breed 'brown' floribundas and I don't like them!

In the middle of one of my shrubberies I have four very tall Scots pines. Some of the shrubs at the moment, as the shrubbery is only six years old, are only half the height of the pines, if that; I have some vigorous Lombardy poplars at one end to screen an electricity pole (made of Scots pine!), and through the poplars in the summer I grow the everlasting sweet pea (white, pink and carmine, one for each poplar). From a distance they really look like flowering Lombardys; and there are two Eucalyptus, nearly twenty feet high. However the pine trunks do stand out rather barely (or did) in spite of the westering sun gilding the red bark. So I put some rambling roses up them; 'Danse de Feu' is one, and a gold and a pink, whose names I forget. But so often in a garden when you have done a particular thing and have had it with you for a couple of years or so, you decide that you can improve on it; and then procrastinate for years before you do it! Well the scheme I hope to get round to is to put up these pine trees a selection of the R. *kordesii*, a line of newish repeat flowering climbing roses. R. *k.* 'Dortmund' is crimson with a white eye, 'Köln am Rhein' deep pink, 'Leunkusen' pale yellow and 'Parkdirector Riggers' a dark velvety red. Now the best thing of all about these *Kordesii* is that the actual flowers stay open for a long time and are weather resisting on their stems, so you get a lot of flowers for a long time.

I am not averse to a shrub border being backed by some rustic work—not wholly—just here and there and particularly if you need to screen an eyesore; and on this rustic work will be climbing roses, clematis and other climbers in season. But this does need special treatment so that you do not lose your natural effect.

JUNE. Back to the shrubbery? We are now into *June*. We have been for some time with the roses. We will start alphabetically with Abelia. I am not growing any at the moment. Only a few are hardy all over the country. They can be evergreen or deciduous. *A. chinensis* is a small shrub with reddish branches and pale green leaves, white and pink flowers, sort of bell-shaped, and flowers late June to July. *A. triflora* is large and erect, flowering in June with white scented flowers in bunches of three.

The Buddleias are very valuable shrubs for producing a quick effect, and indeed some of them will double their height in a year. They can become over-large if used too generously—but they can be propagated so easily and they seed themselves so easily, too, that there is no great drama in yanking one out when you have got tired of it. One of my happiest memories of the bombed sites in London during the war was the speed with which vegetation took over, and one of the commonest plants and quickest growing of all were the self-sown buddleias —sometimes high up a wall—or in the crevice between two walls—sending out, in spite of little root room, great branches 6 ft. long. They are much loved by butterflies and even in these days of sprays and insecticides they bring a galaxy of colourful guests to the garden.

B. globosa is almost evergreen—it is in the south and west— and hardy everywhere. It grows to a large bush up to 15 ft.— it develops in a denser way than the other buddleias—it grows up more than splaying out. In May and June it is covered with orange flowers rather like small oranges or woollen balls which smell richly of honey. I have a seedling which must be a cross from *B. globosa* and *B. davidii* as its racemes are long as in *davidii* but are formed of many little globes—in colour they are a pale silver-mauve tinged with orange or a pale orange with a mauve-silver sheen. I do not know if this cross is a common one—I rather expect so—otherwise my contribution to the garden scene is a *B. globosa × davidii* c.v. 'Fletcher'. But I do not think it will be popular because it goes brown more quickly than any other buddleia flower I know, and this is the sad thing about them. They do die so quickly—or rather go to seed quickly like beautiful actresses who burn the candle at both ends. So I shall not call it 'Betty Astell' who has not, and did not! On second thoughts, I shall not call it 'Fletcher' either—I'm an optimistic type and do not get browned off easily.

Buddleia davidii, from West China, is the popular one; in southern gardens its flowering time begins in June. Up north, perhaps July—but it depends so much always on the position and the soil and the loving care. But a buddleia does not need any of that; it's a robust creature. The flowers are fragrant and range from white through pinks and reds to purples. All strong, dramatic colours. *B. d.* 'Alba' is white; *B. d.* 'Black Knight' has long tapering flowers of deepest violet; *B. d.* 'Charming' is lavender pink; *B. d.* 'Border Beauty'; is more crimson than purple. A sub-species (or different variety might be more correct), *B. d. nanhoensis* has narrower leaves, and a more delicate look altogether has *B. d. n.* 'Pink Pearl', and *B. d. n.* 'Royal Red' is red-purple. For the reddest buddleia of all there is *B. colvilei* which droops its deep rose-red flowers in June, but it is enormous and can grow to 40 ft. —so only for the very largest gardens, please, because if you prune it back every year, as you will have to your other buddleias, you prevent it from flowering. *B. c.* 'Kewensis' is the very reddest of these. But who wants a red buddleia any more than a blue rose or a red daffodil? *B. falloviana* needs cosseting but it is well worth while. It is very fragrant and as a background to its pale lavender flowers it has white felted woolly leaves. For a totally white garden there is *B. f.* 'Alba'—imagine the white panicles against the white felted leaves and stalks. The late Vita Sackville-West had *B. nivea* in her white garden. This has the same white felted leaves and stalks as *B. f.* 'Alba', but surely it has mauve flowers? Perhaps she got up early and nipped them off before anyone was looking! On second thoughts, knowing how much Sir Harold Nicholson, her charming and witty husband, loved her—I expect he did it.

The Crataegus (thorns) are mostly small trees. White trees may flower in May but the red one, *C. oxyacantha* 'Paul's Scarlet' waits with me until June. And waiting is what you have to do when you plant the red one. It will not flower for about five years and nobody seems to tell you this. The haws are always good for colour in the autumn. I hate them in late July because they seem so large and so ready for the autumn and I'm not ready for the autumn in July! Child-like I want my summers to last for ever like they did when I was seven. The scent of May trees is to my mind one of the most 'English' scents there is; it brings the yeoman out in me!

Deutzias are June flowering shrubs. They are most floriferous and there are several double kinds. *D. rosea* 'Carminea' is a compact shrub with ball-shaped pink flowers on arching stems. *D. purpurascens* has white-tinted purple flowers which are scented. You need to thin out old wood after flowering. I find them oddly untidy-looking sometimes.

Erica cinerea flowers from June to September. Only on lime-free soils will you be able to grow *E. c.* 'Alba', pure white, *E. c.* 'Apple Blossom', white with pink, and *E. c.* 'Golden Drop', which has bright golden foliage which turns to russet in winter. '(That's dead', said my mother who is 87 and does not know the ways of heather. 'Why don't you pull it up?') The flowers are pink and very effective against the yellow. *E. cinerea* 'Lilacina' has lilac plants against a bright green foliage. Also *Erica tetralix* is another native heath flowering from June to September but I don't really think heathers—unless they are tree heathers—should be included in the shrubbery. *Erica* × *veitchii* is the hybrid tree heath and the clone is 'Exeter'. It has fragrant white flowers in spring, and you can have it for two or three years and it looks magnificent. Suddenly it's

Plate 6: The gate leading into the midden. Notice the interest given by the different levels and the steps. There is another iron gate leading out the other side

Plate 7 (*top*): This shows how you design the inevitable 'I wonder what is round the corner?' look in a garden. It is the top lawn overlooking the courtyard and facing east

Plate 8 (*bottom*) : More steps—leading up from the courtyard to the level of the tiny yew garden. The pillars are made more of a feature by the urns. The steps have 'matured' more quickly than the actual pillars dead. Heather thrombosis? I must do a whole chapter on heathers.

Escallonia is an evergreen, lime-tolerant and drought resistant. *E.* hybrid variety 'Alice' has bright green polished evergreen leaves and long spikes of rose red blooms. 'Apple Blossom', as in the Ericas, is pink and white. *E. bifida* needs to be protected by a wall and the clone 'Donard Brilliance' has rich pink flowers. 'Crimson Spire' is crimson and used for hedges in the milder areas.

Genistas like a well-drained sunny spot; they will succeed in lime or acid soil. *G. aetnensis* is the Mount Etna broom. It is fast growing up to 15 ft. and has yellow flowers until August. Plant it for best effect against a dark background like a yew hedge and then you will get the effect of a golden fountain. Tiny for the front of the border is *G. delphinensis*. It makes a tight mound of golden flowers until July. *G. pilosa* is a prostrate shrub covered with tiny hairs and is a native.

The hebes used to be called veronicas, and they all come from New Zealand. For this reason not many of them are hardy all over the country but if they commence in June, as some of them do, cut them back after flowering and they will again be generous in September. Some of them come later in the summer but I will discuss all the hardy ones here even though we are supposed to be in June. Shrubs which are spendidly floriferous in August and September are very useful, particularly blue, as these months are so full of reds and yellows: *H.* 'Bowles' Hybrid' is outstanding—a dwarf shrub (for the rock garden really), mauve-coloured and flowers all the summer. It can be 2 ft. high and is very easy to propagate from cuttings. *H. albicans* is dwarf and glaucous; I have it as an edging plant over-flowing a cobbled path and it looks happy. *H. carnea* has long racemes of rose pink flowers. A hebe I saw growing in a tub in a courtyard near one of the Lanes in Brighton looked exotic. I suspect it was, as it had large panicles of lavender blue, *H.* 'Midsummer Beauty'. It needed the stake it had to hold it up—rather as one stakes a fuschia in a tub—and I imagine it would look happiest against (and inland would need the shelter of) a wall facing south or west. *H.* 'Midsummer Beauty' has tan-coloured undersides to its leaves and long lavender spikes of flowers. For seaside gardens and sheltered spots I can recommend *H. speciosa*—deep green shining leaves with a range of colours, reds, purples and blues. *H. s.* 'Cookiana' is white. The bushes grow to 5 ft. high and are covered in blooms.

Hydrangeas come roughly in four kinds. There is the

hydrangea hortensia which is the large mop-head variety, and the Lacecaps which produce a flattened centre to the bloom round which there is a border of ray florets. *H. anomala* and *H. petiolaris* are the climbing hydrangeas which cover vast areas holding on to trees or walls like ivy with aerial roots. The flowers are of the lacecap variety and somewhat insignificant. The plant seems to stand still the first two years and then suddenly it is up and away 10 ft. or more in a season. They love north walls, so are very valuable. The fourth kind is *H. paniculata*—quite a large shrub with large creamy-white flowers a little like syringa but on the ends of the branches, like buddleia. You treat it rather like buddleia by cutting it back in a similar way. With hydrangeas it is important to remember that you should cut back and thin out the old shoots immediately after flowering; it is from this year's new shoots that you will get next year's flowers and if you cut these back you will not get any.

With the hortensias you get large mop-heads of white, pink and blue or glorious subtle combinations of the colours—I'm looking out of the window at a white flower which is shaded slightly here with blue, slightly there with green—like an iceberg in the evening light of April. It is these various colourings which are sometimes of a bronzy metallic kind that make the flowers, when cut and dried at the end of the summer, such good dried winter material for the flower arranger.

A glorious plant, seen to its very best in the woodland garden at Hidcote, is *H. villosa*—the lance-like leaves are green above and white and hairy or felted beneath. It is a blue lacecap; it does require half-shade.

Kalmias, to my mind, are only suitable for south or south-west England and other favoured spots. Then they need to be partially shaded in areas likely to frost, and they need full sun to flower properly. We will have to deny ourselves their splendours. There is *Kalmia latifolia*—the Calico Bush—which is supposed, apart from roses and rhododendrons, to be the best June-flowering shrub. Sickening isn't it! Treat like azaleas or rhododendrons.

Lonicera tellmanniana (it sounds like too much goggle-box!) has flowers of a rich coppery-red and it likes shade. *L. semper-vivens* is evergreen; it's a bit tender so it will be best on a wall—orange-scarlet flowers which look well with the greyish leaves.

Tree Paeonies are not in the least bit like trees, of course, and I am bringing these shrubs to your notice again in June—no morning sun for them please, because of their young foliage, in the early months. Plant them deeply to keep the graft scar well below the surface so that the top part of the graft will grow its own roots.

Magnolia grandiflora is a magnificent evergreen tree which comes into flower in late June and July. It has large long shiny laurel-like leaves and its enormous flowers of ivory-white —8 to 10 in. across—are strongly fragrant. 'Exmouth' is the best known clone. Be very careful if you are growing one against the house (which is undoubtedly the best place for it) that you give it a wide enough border. This applies, too, for all house climbers, like wisterias—otherwise when you use a weed killer on the path adjoining or on the terrace some of the weedkiller may go between the bricks on to the roots of the shrub below the path. The *Magnolia grandiflora* does not grow quickly and if after thirty years you lost one for this reason it would be a tragedy. *M. pyramidata* also blooms in June, so does *M. sieboldii*—with evergreen glaucous leaves and felted undersides, it has white scented flowers with crimson stamens.

Loving scented shrubs, I shall enjoy telling you of the Philadelphus or Mock Orange. This is the shrub which was once called syringa, which is the proper name for lilac. Sorry to rub it in again. They come in all sizes which helps the smaller garden. *P.* 'Belle Etoile' has 2 in. wide flowers—white and flushed maroon. *P. delavayi* 'Nymans' comes from my part of the world, and has grey felted leaves on the underside and pure white flowers. *P.* 'Etoile Rose' has elongated petals of white with a rose colour blotch inside. There are many of them, all flowering in June and July, all fragrant and they range from 3 ft. in height to 8 or 10 ft. You should prune them by thinning out and cutting back immediately after flowering.

Amongst the hybrid rhododendrons for June and July are R. 'Albatross', which is tall-growing with white/pink sweet scented flowers; R. 'Azor', also tall growing with soft salmon-pink flowers with a deeper colour inside; R. 'Britannia' has scarlet-crimson flowers in early June; dark and red is R. 'Dusky Maid'; R. 'Goldsworth Orange' is pale-orange tinged with apricot on a low spreading bush; R. 'Gomer Waterer' is a tall, bushy plant, white with a golden eye; R. 'Iceberg' is tall growing with white sweet scented flowers with a pale crimson blotch at the throat; R. 'Impi' has dark leaves and a very dark maroon red flower; it is of medium height and flowers June/ July. R. 'Mamorata' is the yellow one for June. Succeeding well in the north is R. 'Michael Waterer', crimson. R. 'Purple Splendour' is very hardy and dark purple with a black eye.

I went to Sheffield Park in June when most of the rhododendrons were over—a stupid time to go as their spring display is wonderful—but I'm glad I went then if only for two experiences. Yes, an odd word to use but these were gardening experiences I shall always remember. In the distance of a shady wood, against some darker foliage, possibly of conifer, was this vision of red—the exact red of a huntsman's coat, a 10 ft. high rhododendron with large luminous flowers. It was so aptly named 'Tally-Ho'. The second was an olfactory experience—so far as its pristine flowering period was concerned it was really over—but there was this all-pervading clover smell, one of the sweetest of all scents, and the murmur of innumerable bees. The flowers appear after the leaves, and are funnel-shaped; in colour a silvery-pink and white tipped with a darker pink. The name of this treasure was *Azalea oblongifolium* and it stood, five or six mature plants, each 5 or 6 ft. high, in beds in the grass overlooking one of the lakes. It was a dull, almost misty, day and a day excellent for aroma, and a day when my plane had been held up at Gatwick because of this sort of weather. Livid with irritation at my plans and timings being sent awry I had the happy idea of visiting Sheffield Park, only a few miles away; within a quarter of an hour, walking beside the lakes soaking in the beauty of the plants and trees and the artistry of the planning and planting, I was serenely happy. *Azalea occidentale* is deciduous, fragrant, flowering pale pink, pale orange and yellow, with funnel-shaped flowers in June.

For late-flowering rhododendron species there is R. *auriculatum* with white lily-like flowers of white; R. *decorum,* white tinged with green, and R. *ponticum,* the common purple one which is now nearly a native.

There are no late 'Kurume' azaleas. Of the hybrid Japanese azaleas, there is 'Maerantha', with large red flowers and not very hardy, and 'Naomi', which has pale soft salmon-pink flowers.

Now come the ornamental brambles—perhaps I should include them under climbers: some don't though and are a little like arching, pendulous raspberries. *Rubus biflorus* has white felted leaves underneath and yellow edible berries from white waxy blooms. R. × *fraseri* has fragrant rose-coloured blooms and is useful to grow in shady woodland where naught else will grow.

Spiraea cantoniensis grows to 5 ft. tall and has feathery white flowers and grey-green leaves. *Spiraea japonica* 'Anthony Waterer' has flat, almost yarrow-like, heads of pink or red.

There are various other *S. japonicas,* including *S. j.* 'Fastigiata' which grows in an upright poplar-like way and has very flat white blooms. *S. nipponica* is a lovely sight in June covered with flat white heads borne in clusters.

Styrax japonica is a lovely small tree which has wide spreading fan-like branches and white bell-like flowers in June. It can be a shrub, but as a tree grows to 12 ft.

Syringa—the lilacs of course! *S. villosa* has lilac flowers in June with the underside of the leaves being glaucous, and a relative, *S. wolfii* is pale violet purple with long, almost buddleia-like panicles.

With elm disease about, dare one have a 'Golden' elm? I have mentioned it because at this time of the year as July begins, so the foliage of the trees darken until, in August and September, there is almost a blackness about the oaks. This lovely yellow tree retains its spring-like colour all the summer. Did you know that there is a purple elm? Well, the leaves *are* when young! *Ulmus* × *sarniensis* 'Purpurea'.

There are several viburnums for June and July. *V. betulifolium* grows to 12 ft. and has white flowers in short stemmed clusters with bright red fruits like redcurrants in the autumn. *V. davidii* is 3 ft. evergreen, forming a low mound. The flowers are small and white with bright turquoise-blue fruits in winter. It is therefore more of a winter shrub. *V. japonicum* is an evergreen, medium-sized shrub with white fragrant flowers and red fruits later.

The weigela is a hardy, generous shrub with bell-like flowers and looks like a honeysuckle in the colouring. *W. praecox* starts to flower in May. *W. coraeensis* is white and gets to carmine later. *W. florida* 'Variegata' is a shrub I certainly would never be without—similarly *W. praecox* 'Variegata'—the leaves are a creamy silver-white and this combined with the pink flowers in June is a pretty sight. Both shrubs are so useful for placing between wrong colours, i.e. an orange and a cerise; they are graceful and beautiful in their silvers, growing 6 ft. high at the most. *W.* hybrid 'Mont Blanc' has large white fragrant flowers. Weigelas do tend to die back and leave long curved leafless branches which should be removed, as this keeps the plant tidy.

JULY. Most of the June flowering shrubs continue in variety into July. Fuchsias should be looked at in detail, if only to please that great gardener and television star, Percy Thrower, whose favourite flower it is. I shall only mention ones which have been grown successfully out of doors. Some are often cut by the winter to ground level but they will come again vigorously the next spring. We are all aware of the splendid hedges of fuchsia in Devon and Cornwall, Ireland and Western Scotland, but for less fortunate folk they are so easy to propagate from cuttings that, given a cold frame, you need never be without a whole lot of your favourites ready as understudies (in my profession) or replacements. They don't mind either sun or shade but they do need a well-drained soil. I very much like, and find quite hardy, *F. magellanica* 'Versicolor', which is a small spreading shrub with leaves of a greyish-green which start off by being red. The flowers are scarlet and violet—2 ft. high at the most with me but possibly higher. It is also found in other areas where the winter does not bring it to the ground. *F. procumbens* is a trailer, and *F.* × *bacillaris* 'Display' has large flowers of carmine and rose pink.

Now we will look at lavender, in detail, to please me as it is one of my favourite flowers. Dame Edith Evans says 'It's such a shame when you name your favourite flower—all the others are broken-hearted.' I never cease to wonder at the ease with which lavender will propagate. I have a hedge I have grown from seed—this was in full bloom and size in three seasons—and another by pulling off what I call a 'slip' (which might be a Wiltshire word as I first heard it when I was seven and had my first garden at Trowbridge in Wiltshire), which means a small side shoot pulled off so that it has a 'heel' on it. The top is then pinched out of this shoot and the whole is put into a dull, dampish corner, shoved into the soil which is then firmed well round the shoot—do this in August or April. In three months it will have rooted, and in another three months it will be growing new leaves and shoots. I always have a row of rosemary, santolina, lavender and box cuttings in my kitchen garden—even if I do not need them for 'filling-in' or some new arrangement, I use them as gifts for folk who are starting off a garden. When you start a garden off from absolute scratch, no matter how small it is, there is an awful lot of ground to fill with plants and a kind friend or neighbour with these sorts of gifts eases the pocket of the new gardener no end. This surely is one of the joys of gardening—as your garden matures so your shrubs are large enough to raid for cuttings and so in the odd corner here and there—especially on the paths there will be this multitude of seedlings. If you are like me, you cannot bear to throw them away—so I dibble them in in the odd corner, perhaps to increase my own stock, or perhaps to give away. Sometimes, in the way of my buddleia, the seedling may be new and interesting—or it may be quite inferior when it does flower, in which case you must be hard-hearted and throw it away, as an inferior plant takes up as much room and needs as much loving care as a superior one. So do not on any account bother with it.

Whilst I am digressing in this way—and this is not really going to be all that out of place because, after all, we are planting our shrubbery—try to strive after what I call a haphazard luxuriance. Or a cultivated wildness if you need another contradiction of terms! This is where Nature very frequently scores again and again —she will put, quite by accident, a seedling just where you, at first thought, would never dream of putting it, and it gives just that added nonchalant effect of making the garden look less contrived. I see a good gardener as someone who is using and guiding and bending Nature in a completely unnatural way to create a picture which, when whole and finished (as if you will ever finish!) looks like a natural work of art. How can it be natural—you will have a shrub from Chile next to one from Formosa; a half-hardy annual (sub-tropical) next to a flower from the highest Alps or the bleakest Tundra—and no bare earth, I beg of you—rather have ten plants struggling for room and light and sustenance than large bare expanses of earth.

Lavender I was saying! *Lavandula,* which word is from the Romans who used lavender in the bath, and it comes from *lavo,* to wash! Lavenders come from the Mediterranean countries. *L. lanata* is the whitest and woolliest of them all; it flowers from July to September and comes from Spain. *L. spica* is the ordinary common or garden lavender. It has many varieties: *L. s.* 'Alba', with white flowers—I have got it in my white garden but it seems to grow more slowly than the others. *L. s.* 'Hidcote' is a compact plant with a very floriferous habit and dark lavender spikes; it seems to go on longer than others. *L. s.* 'Nana Alba' is white and minute and could be used on the rockery. There is also a pink one, *L. s.* 'Loddon Pink' and from Gertrude Jekyll's garden we have *L. s.* 'Munstead', blue lavender, and *L. s.* 'Nana Munstead Dwarf' is excellent for a low edging round a bed—particularly round a rose bed which you have mulched with lawn mowing— it stops the birds leaving all the litter on the paths. All you do with lavender is to trim off the dead flowers and tidy the bush or hedge at the same time. Also, do have some spares handy, as sometimes, just when all the bushes are the same height and you are very pleased with the look of them, one bush will collapse and die. This happens in very dry summers and you must have a replacement handy. It helps if you see one shoot has died—have it off before the bush decides to follow suit. There is a farming saying which is that the best manure on the farm is the farmer's boot, meaning if he keeps going around he can see things happening, and can take advantage of them. So it is with gardeners—keep walking round; you are not being lazy—you are noticing and acting on what you find. If your garden is large go around with a notebook. You will be surprised what you forget.

Tree paeonies we have had; now please regard the Tree Poppy. They are from California so they need a warm, sunny position. *Romneya coulteri* has deeply cut foliage which is grey-green; the flowers are large and white with yellow stamens. I read that they take a long time to establish but once they have done this their roots spread underground with great rapidity. Mine hasn't. Mine might be R. *c.* × *hybrida* 'White Cloud'. I think I shall have to move it. (Gets note-book out!)

AUGUST. Most of the *July* shrubs are represented by August flowering varieties. An important shrub to flower now is the Caryopteris because it is blue and the garden does tend to go to yellows, oranges and reds in August. Caryopteris also has aromatic leaves and, by now, you will know that this recommends a plant doubly to me. *C. incana* is my favourite because it is a grey-leaved plant and this, with the blue flowers, is most attractive. A shrub up to 6 ft. in height is *C. clandonensis*, with grey-green leaves and deep lavender-blue flowers, the best hybrid clone being 'Arthur Simmonds'—this flowers more freely than *C. incana*. Ceanothus, another blue shrub, obliges again in August.

The hibiscus is very useful in late summer. It is in effect a shrubby mallow, often called the Tree Hollyhock, and the flowers are very like the annual lavateria—it is eventually a large-sized shrub but it is certainly slow to get started. *H. syriacus* is the usual variety seen—I have three, one pink, 'Duc de Brabant', *H. s.* 'Totus Albus', which has large, single, white flowers, and *H. s.* 'Coelestis', with single blue flowers.

Hypericum—the shrubby St John's Wort—is a valuable contribution to the late summer scene. It is most floriferous with large butter-cup yellow flowers. *H. calycinum*—the 'Rose of Sharon'—is an excellent ground-cover plant and can be used in full sun or shade—to my mind, although it is the most despised and commonest of the St John's Worts—its flower is the largest and most beautiful. Trim it lightly in the spring.

H. elatum—the 'Elstead' variety—has several small flowers at the end of each stem. *H. kalmianum* is attractive in that its flower almost entirely consists of the anthers and the petals are small in comparison. I find this most attractive. There are about thirty or so different varieties—all with yellow flowers, all hardy and most flowering at this time of year. There is a small one, *H. empetrifolium*, which is a prostrate shrub suitable for the rock garden.

The myrtles are aromatic evergreens which need a mild climate. They are fragrant evergreens, usually white. I loved one which grew (still does, I hope) by the bridge of a water wheel in Devon. This would have been *Myrtus communis*—an aromatically dark-leaved shrub, with white flowers in July and August. I took a cutting which grew but died outside in a Sussex winter. *M. cheken* is reckoned the hardiest.

In October, November and December we come around to the winter shrubs already described like the mahonias, viburnums, ericas, winter jasmine, *hamamelis, lonicera*, etc.

In the winter, one has to depend on the evergreens and, in particular, the conifers to clothe the garden. It is right then that we should now look a little longer and in more detail at the conifers.

10 Conifers

I have already discussed the importance of coniferous trees and shrubs in the design of gardens—how, because of their varied colours and the fact that most of them are evergreen, or ever-blue or ever-yellow, they will become the permanent framework of the garden and will feature as the exclamation marks here and there. The garden, like every other work of art, should have a climax or focus of attention and this is sometimes provided better by a splendid and specimen conifer than by some costly but out-of-scale and period fountain, folly or sundial.

We have also discussed conifers as hedges and ground cover, and the tiny ones which are suitable for rock gardens.

Conifers are often mass-produced by nurseries and sent out —particularly if you are attracted by a very cheap price—in poor condition and poor quality. The symmetry of a conifer is all-important and frequently cannot be remedied by pruning, as it can with a deciduous tree. The shape and form of the new tree is to be with you for a lifetime and, for this reason, it is far better for you to go to a reputable nursery or garden centre in person to choose your own specimens. It is important that all conifers should have foliage at the base of the plant.

Conifers should be planted in early autumn whilst the ground is still warm and the air is sufficiently cool not to allow transpiration, or in the spring when the soil has warmed a little. There is more danger in the spring of a shrub drying out with cold, drying winds or with hot sunshine and you must be very busy with the watering can, not only on the roots but twice daily if necessary over the whole plant with a fine rose attached to the watering can. There are also various proprietary sprays which will lock the moisture in your plant and stop transpiration.

Complete conifer gardens may be grown (as one has an iris or rose garden), grouped amongst grass, and possibly heathers, the various shapes, sizes, textures and species giving not only pleasure when growing but great joy in arranging; this shape against that shape, and this colour next to that colour, almost more with conifers than any other plant, as the colour is there and you are not waiting for blossom. For those with small gardens one of the joys of the conifer is that so many of them are slow growing.

Conifers are not fussy as to soil; some, like the junipers, thrive on thin soils—some, like the yews flourish in chalk. I have proved in my quick-growing *lawsoniana* hedges that an addition of well-rotted cow manure and compost will give your plants a good start. You will have that two years settling in period and then suddenly woosh! The humus you have provided gives the extra boost needed, not only for growth but for colour and general healthy-lookingness.

Conifers are often used as screens against noise—either of traffic or neighbours or children in schools or the odd abattoir. If you decide on a conifer screen, then they are best planted in two rows with the plants alternating with the spacing and the two rows sufficiently far apart for the future size of the trees. Planted this way the noise is absorbed.

Here now are the main groups of conifers you will use. The variety is going to be such a personal choice that I cannot really advise and will not give a long list with specifications. (What I can do is to recommend a gloriously illustrated book with 150 pages of coloured pictures—which are so good you could choose your actual plants from it—*Conifers for your Garden* by Adrian Bloom and published by Floraprint Ltd).

Abies are the fir trees; there are many forest giants in these species but there are plenty of small ones and medium-sized ones, too.

Cedrus: The cedars, to my mind the most beautiful of all. Alas, they are slow-growing and if you plant one on your lawn and anticipate eating cucumber sandwiches from a silver salver brought to you by the family butler in the shade of it, then your wait will be forty years at least. *Cedrus atlantica* 'Glauca' is the most beautiful, and a ten-year-old specimen is as beautiful in a smaller garden as a 40 ft. specimen is in a park.

Chamaecyparis—the new name for *cupressus*—has about forty or so popular species used in the garden today. Tall, pyramid-shaped, columnar, creeping, blue, golden, green, yellow, variegated—indeed all shapes, sizes, and colours. There is even *Chamaecyparis lawsoniana* 'Fletcheri'; he is broadly columnar (a critic of my gardening programme described me as portly!) with greyish-green foliage of a small pleasing texture.

It grows quite slowly but will eventually make a tall shrub of 10 ft.—mine is now about 5 ft. and has grown to this from 2 ft. in seven years. A grafted plant will grow larger and one taken originally as a cutting will only grow to about 5 ft. I have *C. l.* 'Pygmaea Argentia' as the 'stop' plant on a dry wall one side of some steps in my 'midden' garden—this with its silvery white tips and deeper inner glow of darker green is beautiful to behold. *C. l.* 'Stewartii' is the most breathtaking of the goldens.

Cryptomeria japonica is a feathery foliaged species which has bright green foliage which turns brown or bronze in the winter. It likes moist soils and there are many kinds. Most of us choose *C. j.* 'Elegans'.

The *Cupressus,* now separated by the botanists from the *Chamaecyparis*—perhaps I should have written it the other way round—has amongst its cultivars the *C. leylandii* which is the wonder quick-growing plant—once settled in, it will grow 2 to 3 ft. a year.

The Junipers are natives of the Northern Hemisphere, and the *Juniperus communis* is a native of this land and does equally well on lime or acid soils. Its berries are blackish-blue and the oil from the unripe berries is the flavour given to gin. There are little sentinel junipers and lovely creeping blue junipers (*J. horizontalis* 'Glauca') and pencil-thin ones like *J. scopulorum* 'Skyrocket'. All are hardy and quite possibly the most useful group of conifers. *J. squamata* 'Meyeri' is another of my favourites which is very effective in a mixed border against a purple berberis.

The *Larix* are the larches—not evergreen—and in autumn when the needle-leaves turn golden and droop so gracefully you think it is the most beautiful tree you have ever seen. Then in the spring with the daintiest and brightest green needles emerging in tufted bunches you think that it is at its most beautiful then. They grow quite quickly and to my mind need to be in a little cluster of four or five rather than on their own.

Picea are the spruces. Here again there are large and small and some very attractive dwarf cultivars. One of the bluest of all conifers is *P. pungens* 'Prostrata'.

Then there are the pines (*Pinus*). Again with such very attractive miniatures and compact forms.

Taxodium distichum is the Swamp Cypress. There is an enormously graceful specimen tree in the courtyard at Dartington Hall. I have a minute one on the island of a tiny pond.

Taxus is the yew. *Taxus baccata* is the English yew so favoured as a hedge plant. There are variegated and golden cultivars and the Irish yew, *Taxus baccata* 'Fastigiata'.

Thuja is a genus similar in some ways to *Chamaecyparis* and it comprises about a dozen species. *Thuja plicata* is the Western Red Cedar and we use it widely in this country for hedges. It doesn't seem to mind clipping. Here again, there are many cultivars, large and small. *Thuja* 'Rheingold' is a dwarf cultivar with most attractive feathery golden foliage in summer, becoming bronze in winter.

I envy those of you who have mature gardens planted perhaps fifty or sixty years ago with magnificent specimen conifers in them. I think it is wrong not to plant them for your children to enjoy; with inheritance taxed as it is today, there is little continuity in the possessions we have and the possessions we leave. In these days we are an itinerant lot. I myself have had five gardens in my thirty odd years of marriage. If one says to oneself there is little likelihood of my successors enjoying these trees which I am planting, when they mature, at least they will add to the value of my property when I sell or die.

I'd give anything to have that one hundred-year-old cedar on my lawn!

11 Herbaceous Borders

Herbaceous borders mean, to the older gardener, borders about 15 ft. wide on either side of a grass path which is, perhaps, 10 ft. wide—the whole possibly 100 ft. long and finishing in a large ornamental seat or piece of statuary. Each border will be backed by a yew hedge or a wall. Old fashioned, beautiful and time-consuming as they are if you see a good example of one—Hilliers' Garden near Winchester has a splendid example, and so had the late Hon. Mrs Ionides at Buxted Park—they are superb and make the beholder long to be the proud owner of one. The same can be said of the long border at Dixter which is a wide border on one side of a stone-flagged path.

At the turn of the century Gertrude Jekyll was advocating mixed borders—herbaceous plants and shrubs—and to this I would add bulbs in season and in their right place, annuals and half hardy annuals, and rhizomes like dahlias (only dahlias are tubers!). Now suddenly like a breath of fresh air we have that great gardener Alan Bloom advocating from his lovely gardens at Bressingham that we should have herbaceous borders again, but this time he calls them hardy perennials and advocates that they should be in island beds.

The chief drawback to herbaceous borders or hardy perennial beds, or call them what you will, is their utter unsightliness in winter. Mr Bloom in his marvellous book *Perennials for your Garden* published by Bressingham Gardens Ltd, says that in his garden he has his first flowers in February and his last in December. He may do, but I am sure that he has hummocks of deadish looking plants as well, which in a mixed border are hidden—or your eyes are distracted away from—by bright conifers and evergreen shrubs which give an interest and a shape to your border or island site in the winter. In winter especially, if you have not got it, you must try and cultivate a joy in the shapes of things, the varieties of texture, the symmetry of nature, and seek pleasure out of the difference in the shape of this leaf or that leaf. Know and delight in the beauty of a shaft of winter light—or a summer's evening light with misty motes of dust in it—shining on the silvery side of a particular plant or the golden lacquer of a leaf. Enjoy and revel in the scents of a garden and in the animation of trees in the wind.

After that most important digression, where have I got to? What kind of a border to have? A mixed one with a bit of everything to give you form and delight throughout the year or a purely perennial one—preferably as an island bed containing the newer, hardier kinds of herbaceous plants advocated, and in many cases bred, by Alan Bloom.

No plant can be adapted to accept every kind of position in a garden. Some need shade, some damp, some dry, some sun, some need to be baked and some need particular shelter. All of this we can contrive by siting our borders and beds in different places and choosing the plants we need. Mr Bloom suggests wisely that we need only use plants which do not require staking (a terrible time consumer in the old-style borders), which have long periods of flower and which are hardy all over the country. In an island bed the plant has more air and sun and is healthier. It is not drawn-up by a backing hedge, neither does the hedge rob the taller plants of a lot of necessary food.

Island beds of unconventional shapes, not necessarily flat shapes either—the bed can slope from the centre outwards, or from the back downwards towards you—will cure at last that oblong piece of grass which I see from the train so often and which always looks so very dreary. You can see your plants from all sides in an island bed. Also you have easier access to them. From all sides to the middle being perhaps half the distance from the front to the back hedge of the old border. You need to space craftily using the centre of the bed for the highest plants and the edges for the shorter ones, and as in the old border you do need to use several plants of one variety in a mass to avoid a spotty effect.

A very important point to remember when planning your border is not only to place each group of plants correctly for height, colour and season; you will also need to bear in mind the fact that whilst one variety of plant will be very vigorous, its neighbour may perhaps be delicate and a slower grower. It could then be overwhelmed by its neighbour. Correct planting and planning prevents this.

Do not use just any old awkward bit of the garden for your island beds. Give them a good chance, although it is always a challenge to use plants designed by nature (and sometimes by man) for the exigencies of their situations. Yes, there are even plants which cope beautifully with dry shade! And plenty which will not!

When you think of all the necessary factors to be considered—height, length of flowering, time of flowering, shade or sun loving, dry or damp loving, lime or acid loving, slow or quick growing, shy or overpowering, contrasting and blending of colour, you will see that it is an absolute necessity to make a plan. Graph paper gives you an immediate and ready scale, a rubber will help your second thoughts.

Every nurseryman and every gardening book will give you plans for an herbaceous border with areas marked out and filled with the names of the flower and its variety and clone. But they do not know your conditions of soil, your climatic conditions and your personal likes and dislikes of some plants and some colours. I am afraid therefore that you will have to make this plan for yourself. Have an india rubber please and infinite patience and have, too, when June and July come round that creative glow of satisfaction as you feast your contented eye one early evening on the results of your handiwork.

I am going to assume that you know all the cottage flowers. All the flowers which have delighted the owners of 'Mon Repos' or 'Dunrovin' for years. I shall make a list of them and then I will make a list and some notes of the more modern forms of some plants which are not quite such well known favourite as those sin the first list. We know we are going to use members of the first list because they will consist of such plants as *Anemone japonica*, the tall pink and white ones which flower in late summer and autumn; aquilegia—some lovely new varieties from seed; asters—the Michaelmas daisies, *amellus* and *novi-belgii* and *novi-angliae*, tall ones and dwarf ones—the dwarf and newer shorter ones are most useful because they require no staking; cornflowers (but I'll go into these in detail later because of the new ones); summer chrysanthemums like 'Esther Read'; delphiniums (Yes, Madam, you *will* have to stake these and well worth it they are too—get Langdon and Blackmore's Catalogue, go mad and buy beds full of them, every blue and grey and white one there is—but not a pink one I implore you—who ever heard of a pink delphinium? 'The Hero looked into her wide open eyes of delphinium pink!'; dianthus—pinks of all kinds; gaillardias—those glorious red and yellow daisies with blood pressure; geraniums—no, not the bedding out pelargonium variety but the Cranesbill type,

Plate 9: Looking from the top of the steps shown in Plate 8 to the courtyard in front of the house, spacious enough for several cars to park and also turn round. If there is space, make sure you give enough room for this

Plate 10: The long walk in the spring, looking east from the terrace

pinks and blues; get *G. macrorrhizium,* whose leaves smell of sweet briar when crushed. Geums, heleniums, the late summer gold and mahogany daisies; iris (I'd dearly like to have a little garden for these all on their own with gladioli planted amongst them for a later season's flowering); red-hot pokers; lupins (do have the named clone Russell lupin 'Betty Astell'— it's a lovely pink and vigorous); paeonies—get Messrs Kelways Catalogue and have a mouth-drooling session with it. Then order some and enjoy their scent. It is subtle and sweet and full of nectar. The paeony needs no staking; you must leave it where it is as it resents disturbance, do not plant the crowns too deeply and make sure you order *P.* var. 'Jules Elie' which is a delicate silvery rose and fully double, and 'La France' which is pink double but showing delicate anthers of gold.

Papaver are the oriental poppies. Then comes the phlox—there are some wonderful new varieties: *Phlox paniculata* 'Admiral' which is pure white; *P. p.* 'Starfire'—a royal purple; *P. p.* 'Prince of Orange'—which is orange; and *P. p.* 'Sandringham', a lovely pink with a darker eye. *P. p.* 'Hampton Court' is blue. Eel worm is their particular pest and badly affected plants must be dug up and burned and the ground not used for phlox for three years. They are especially good for late summer when there is too much yellow about in the border.

Primulas you'll know. *Primula vulgaris* is the primrose and, I often think, the most perfect flower of all. Its leaf is attractive, its scent is lovely, it has the charm to flower early when we most need it, and it has an innocent look about it that makes the world seem cleaner! Many of the primulas need damp.

Pyrethrum, the red, pink or white daisy with ferny foliage and single or double flowers, likes lime and well-drained soil. *Scabiosa* (scabious) prefer a chalky soil and there are some lovely blue, white and lavender varieties. You should divide them every three or four years. There is a species *S. graminifolia* which is a dwarf and flowers from June to September. Golden Rod (*Solidago*) we have all known for ever, but there are many new varieties today. They are shorter, bushier and showier, some being as short as 12 in. *Stachys lanata*—or Lamb's Lugs is a beautiful grey carpeter, in the variety *S.* 'Silver Carpet'—it only spreads and does not flower. I like the flowers when they are young and downy but you do have to keep a watch on them as they go to seed rather inelegantly. Verbascums or the Mulleins are well known enough for this preliminary list. They have a very effective 4 ft. spike of yellow flowers from June to August. There are several kinds, *V.* 'Gainsborough' is pale yellow with grey felt for leaves. They are tap-rooted so will not divide. *V. hartleyi* has yellow and purple flowers in 5 ft. spikes. Sow the seed out of doors in May for plants to flower the following year, since it is best to use them as a biennial. Since I have included verbascums in this list I should perhaps also have put in Anchusa, from 3 to 4 ft. high. *A.* 'Morning Glory' likes well-drained winter soil and has bright blue forget-me-not-like flowers from June to September. You increase them from basal cuttings or root cuttings. You have to do this, since this prolific plant will exhaust itself after three seasons. The flowers are edible and fun to put in a salad; they look amusing in ice cubes for drinks too.

Now let us go through the list of better-known hardy perennials which are right for island beds as well as mixed borders. It is indeed necessary to know one species from another and not to get our exotics mixed up—rather as the small child did who, seeing Za Za Gabor come out of a West End Store, cried: 'Look, Mummy—there's Danny La Rue!'

Achillea flipendulina 'Gold Plate' reaches 4½ ft. in height and needs a few pea sticks amongst it. It carries the same flowers from June to August and the leaves are fern-like and beautiful. *A.* 'Moonshine' is only 30 in. high and has silvery foliage and pale yellow flowers—it is also compact. *A. millefolium* 'Cerise Queen' is pink and the blooms grow from a mat of foliage which needs looking after. Indeed all the yarrows need to be looked at every two or three years. Give some away or you will be inundated. There is a tall one with separate white button-like flowers called 'The Pearl'. It does need staking and is a good subject for a white garden.

ACANTHUS, otherwise known as Bear's Breeches. Heaven knows why! Its leaves are thistle-like and its flowers are spiny. The leaves have inspired the design on Corinthian pillars and is much used in Georgian classical architectural motifs. Liking either sun or shade, *A. spinosus* is a vigorous expanding plant with very long lasting spire-like flowers of dark mauve and white, up to 4 ft. in height. It is a spectacular plant with deep fleshy roots. It seeds easily with me and I'm always finding new corners for plants—I could not bear to give or throw it away, so beautiful and unusual is it.

Alchemilla mollis has a nondescript yellowish flower from June to August of sulphur yellow, but it is very accommodating, liking a dry position. It is good ground cover in a poor soil or awkward corner.

ACONITUM (we know them as Monkshoods) are named from the Greek *akon*: a dart. The juice of this plant is poisonous so if you want poisoned arrows here is the very thing. They don't mind sun or shade, they have tuberous roots and are related to the delphinium. Aconitum have a long flowering season and need mulching. *A.* 'Bressingham Spire' has a symmetrical violet-blue spike 3 ft. high, from July to September. From June to August *A. napillus* 'Bicolor' has flowers of white and shaded blue 3 to 3½ ft. tall, and is good for shade. *A. fischeri* is a good late one and comes from North America. Its flowers are like a broad blue helmet. *A. n.* 'Album' is white. Also ivory white is *A.* 'Ivorine', 3 ft. high and it flowers from May to July. This is a useful time to have white in the border.

AGAPANTHUS. The African Lily or Lily of the Nile used to be reckoned half-hardy and was kept in tubs and trundled in and out of the cold greenhouse. Its blue lily-like flowers are borne from July to September. It is 2–3 ft. tall and likes moisture in the growing season. The modern varieties *A.* 'Isis' and *A.* 'Profusion' are hardy. They are used to great effect in tubs along the middle of the road near the Princess Theatre at Torquay.

The ALLIUMS are onions—so do not step on the foliage! *A. acuminatum* has rose-purple flowers in June and is 1 ft. high. *A. caeruleum* is 3 ft., and flowers from May to June. *A. giganteum* has immense globular heads of pink flowers on 4 ft. stems, May to June. They grow in profusion at Great Dixter and I was very struck with them.

ANAPHALIS has silver leaves with many small white tufted little flowers held at the top of the stem, rather like the way in which the Sweet William holds its flowers. It does not mind dry shade and is good ground cover. I like the tallest one *A. yedoensis,* which is 2–2½ ft. high and flowers from July onwards. The flowers, cut at the end of the summer, can be dried for arrangements. It is a superb plant for a white and grey garden. Drummond Castle in Perthshire has a double border of this plant in the form of an enormous Cross of St. Andrew, hundreds of yards long—a spectacular sight!

ALSTROEMERIA 'Ligtu hybrids'. This is the Peruvian Lily. It needs a deep sandy soil and the fleshy roots should be 12 in. beneath the soil. Once established—and it takes about a year (plant it in a group preferably shaded by a wall)—it is a great sight with its many colours ranging from white through yellow to red with sometimes lilac and rose-purple. You need to decide where it is to go and then plant from pots or seed, which you plant 1 in. deep, then leave it to establish itself. Year after year this galaxy of colour will flower from June to September. It is not really suitable for an island bed.

ARTEMESIA belongs to a group of plants which are largely woody and rejoice in the name of Mugwort—Oliver Cromwell fans please come forward! *Artemesia* 'Lambrook Silver' is a lovely plant if you never allow it to flower! By this I mean the flowers are insignificant and the foliage is very beautiful. A dry, sunny position is best for most silver leaved plants. *Artemesia lactiflora* has off-white plumes on erect stalks about 4 ft. high. The leaves are beautiful in themselves and the plant does not need staking.

ARMERIA is the thrift, and I should have included it in the list of more common plants. There are some good new varieties, *A. maritima* 'Vindictivi', and *A. m.* 'Alba-white'. There is also *A.* 'Ruby Glow'. But 'Bees Ruby' is gigantic for a thrift, with 18 in. stems and large mop-heads of deep pink. I am not sure I want my thrift that high, I'd rather grow chives which look the same and are useful for the pot!

Aruncus sylvester is a noble plant which needs a good, important position and lots of room. Very much a mixed border plant I would say, but I can see that it would make a magnificent centre plant for an island bed. It can be 6 ft. high, and it likes damp and shade. Again, the flowers are feathery and plume-like with leaves shaped like a rambler rose, only bigger.

ASTRANTIA I had not met, until one day we did a TV show from the herbaceous borders of King's Heath Park, Birmingham. It was a close, cloudy day with impending thunder and the scent from the flowers was quaint and strong and very pleasant. To me it was a new 'flavour' as it were, coming from a somewhat disappointing flower. *A. maxima* it was, about $2\frac{1}{2}$ ft. high, with mauvish, reddish, whitish flowers. I have looked it up in several books and no one mentions the perfume—do you think it was the camera-man's after shave?

Aster frikarti has blue flowers rather like a Michaelmas Daisy but it goes on and on and on, flowering from early July till the end of the season. It is too generous a plant for you not to have a large mass of it. When it dies down in the winter it completely disappears, so mark it well if you have a new gardener, or he will do for it as one of mine did.

The ASTILBES are very lovely cultivated variations of the native meadow sweet. This grows in ditches so astilbes do need moisture, or a damp, shady place. They range from white, through pink to darkest red. They vary in height from 4 in. to 6 ft. They flower during June. Do try some, but in a dry summer make sure they remain moist.

BERGENIAS, which Gertrude Jekyll called *Megasea ligulata*, and which she very much favoured. She considered them good company for the hellebores (Christmas roses), and so do I. They will grow under trees where it is fairly dry, but their leaves in these conditions, and their progress, is about half that when in the sun. They produce their pink flowers on thick fleshy stalks and the leaves are large and opulent (like elephants' ears someone said). *B. cordifolia* 'Purpurea' is 15 in. high, is the most common Bergenia and has purple-bronzy leaves. The Germans have gone to town and produced some good new cultivars, *B.* 'Abendglut' (dwarf), 'Morgenrote', and there is a white one, 'Silberlicht'.

CATANANCHE has grass-like leaves and blue cornflower-like flowers, from June to September. It is 2 ft. high and likes sun and well-drained soil. *C. caerulea* has greyish-green leaves, and the flowers can be dried for the winter.

CAMPANULAS could have a chapter all of their own. They usually are blue (sometimes white) of all shades, shapes and sizes and heights. They don't mind sun or shade, and they are most liberal in increase by division. The short one for borders is *C. carpatica*; it is 6–12 in. in height and can be white or blue. This plant, with mop-head hydrangeas, is grown to distraction on the Isle of Wight. I was there for three years with my Summer Show, and I find it difficult on looking back to remember any other flowers. In July flowers *C. persicifolia* with 3 ft. spires of open bell-shaped bright blue. There is *C. p.* 'Alba' a white one, and *C. p.* 'Verdun', a violet-blue one; it spreads. *C. glomerata* 'Superba', is aptly described by its botanical name, which means 'clustered'. It has large heads of clustered violet-blue flowers and looks totally unlike any of the others, whose bells are mostly up their stems, except *C. lactiflora,* which has looser sprays of open funnel-shaped flowers, originally of white tinged with blue (hence *lactiflora*—milky). But *C. l.* 'Pritchard's variety' is lavender-mauve. *C. lactiflora* will grow up to 5 ft. in height, and self-sown seedlings help you to keep this plant going, as it is not long-lived. However, sometimes the seedlings will fall too near the front of your border for true happiness, so you need to cut this straying bell flower down to about a foot above ground at the beginning of June; you will then have a flowering mass 2 ft. in height, which will bloom at the same time as its parents and can be moved back home with them in the autumn. You can do this with other plants such as Michaelmas daisies, and even tall annuals such as sunflowers—though I don't fancy one of those large heads looking up at me from 3 ft. instead of down on me from nine. On second thoughts not sunflowers!

Campanula latifolia 'Gloaming' is my favourite. It has spires— 4 ft. of pale lilac-blue. The shape of the spire is so beautiful with the flowers all round both it and the tip, with the buds slender and delicate. Its rapidity of growth is amazing. It is good for the shady part of the border but it's just as good in the sun. This plant is a *must* for every border.

The cornflowers and sweet sultans, well-known to us as annuals, and the wild flower knapweed, have relatives: the CENTAUREAS, which are ideal for the perennial border, and all need sun. Cornflower blue you would think, but the most spectacular ones are 6–8 ft. high, *C. babylonica,* with large silvery-white leaves and loose sprays of yellow flowers. *C. macrocephala* has large yellow thistle-like heads, is 5 ft. high and flowers from June to August on short stems. It is good for association with shrubs. *C. montana* is the common kind with silvery-green leaves. *C. dealbata* 'Steenbergii' has deep pink flowers in June and July. 'Dealbata' means white-washed, and refers to the white centre of the flower, and the white edges. I noted a mauve cornflower at Hidcote—which was outstanding in late August. Alas, there was no name plate, or I could not find one. Was it perhaps *C. gymnocarpa,* as it had intensely silver leaves and small violet flowers? Someone write and put me out of my misery; I'd love to own it.

COREOPSIS is usually an annual—or treated as an annual. They like the sun. *C.* 'Grandiflora' has large yellow daisy-like leaves on long stems, about 2½ ft. in height. *C. lancelota* is like 'Grandiflora' but is a proper perennial.

Crocosmia masonorum is a monbretia-type plant with red flowers on 2½ ft. stems in mid-summer. It has been introduced by Alan Bloom of Bressingham Gardens.

DICENTRA is the 'Bleeding Heart' plant with fern-like leaves. *Dicentra spectablis* is the one popularly grown. It has a long flowering period from May and, I think, looks well in a high-up corner of a rockery or dry wall, so that you can see it from underneath.

DIANTHUS—the pinks. One immediately thinks of the white pink 'Mrs Sinkins' with her double flowers bursting from their calyx—but she, deservedly popular as she still is, is by no means alone today. Do get a catalogue of dianthus from Allwoods,

102

and you will be amazed at the varieties and strains, shapes, sizes and colours. Some small 'alpine' pinks are very good for the border. And so are the border carnations or clove pink *D. caryophyllus*. Then there is the 'Allwoodii', the modern perpetual flowering pink, 9–12 in. high; Tudor Lace pinks, which have unusual markings largely round the edges; Sweet Wivelsfield which I believe is a cross between the pinks and the Sweet William (also a dianthus). When we lived in the Water Mill at Colemans Hatch on the edge of the Ashdown Forest in Sussex, we had a bed of these tiny, jewel-like plants, just near to the 'cat-hole' in the door of the mill building through which, one summer, came tumbling in and out six beautiful long-haired kittens—in and out of the door and in and out of the Sweet Wivelsfield they would play in the sun. I never see these flowers without thinking of the flower-like faces of those innocent little balls of fur. *Dianthus* 'Betty Norton' is an old fashioned single pink, with large deep rose flowers with maroon eyes; she flowers from May to September. *D. deltiodes* 'Flashing Light', makes a carpet of foliage which flowers from June to August with a myriad of bright cerise-red blooms. All pinks and border carnations can be increased by cuttings or divisions, or by layering in the autumn. The singles come easily from seed.

I do not grow doronicums, as they are yellow daisies which flower early in the year when there is a mass of yellow flowers about. But I welcome with open arms the ERIGERONS, daisies which flower from June to August. There are many new varieties of erigeron these days—the plants old name was fleabane. They are largely June flowering. 'Charity' is light pink with finely rayed flowers, 2 ft. high. 'Darkest of All' is very upright with deep violet-blue flowers. 'Dignity' is mauve-blue. 'Foersters Liebling' is a double deep cerise-pink, with small flowers and very upright (2 ft.). This is the one to have. There are also 'Wuppert!hal', pale amethyst-blue, a large semi-double at 2½ ft. and 'Quakeress', white, 2 ft. 'Gaiety' is deep pink, cuts well and is 2 ft. tall.

ECHINOPS is the globe thistle. It flowers from June onwards. *E. humilis* 'Taplow Blue' has dark-blue globes and grows to 5 ft., and *E. ritro* has rich blue globes and is very good at 3 ft.

ERYNGIUM is easily confused with the globe thistle—it is in fact the sea holly, which is ideal for winter decorations. *E. tripartitum* has metallic blue flowers and silver-grey foliage, and is 3 ft. 'Blue Dwarf' is similar. 'Spring Hills', 3 ft., has deep blue thistles, 'Jewel' is violet and *E. planum* (4 ft.) has masses of small blue flowers in branching sprays. *E. variefolium* has pretty marbled foliage near the ground, and erect branches of blue flowers at 2½ ft.

EUPHORBIA is the spurge—and it is one of these, the Caper Spurge (*E. lathyrus*) that is supposed to repel moles. We mentioned this on the TV show and had many enquiries about it. At that time of the year (about February), I was having terrible trouble on my lower lawn which is nearest to one of my fields, and has but a beech hedge and some wire netting between it and the mole-ridden field. So I brought the plant home that we had showed on the programme. No sooner had I planted it than the mole hills in the lawn completely departed. My usual procedure up to then had been that daily I would drop a little petrol down the hole and stamp back all the soil into it very vigorously, as I had heard that moles disliked vibrations! Well as if by magic, the Caper Spurge having been planted: no new holes. All summer through, no new holes! Until last week when there was a mole hill one foot from the plant, which made me laugh. Next day I was hysterical. The mole had made a mound immediately underneath the plant and had it half out of the ground. The three dogs— my English Setter, Cocker Spaniel and Jack Russell terrier, then decided, when I wasn't looking, to 'have a go', and the lawn is now like Mons battlefield, and at the moment the mole is inactive. So in spite of Mr Shewell-Cooper's correspondence in this plant's favour in the *Daily Telegraph* all I can say is that my moles in Sussex must possess ossified olfactory organs as well as a sense of humour.

Euphorbia cyparissias is good for a dry spot and is 6 in. high. *E. griffithii* (2 ft.) has orange-red flowers. *E. polychroma* (*epithymoides*) has lemon-green flowers from February onwards. At 18 in. it is a spectacular flower which I adore. *E. wulfenii* is shrubby and will grow in a dry soil up to an imposing 3 ft. Incidentally, *Euphorbia pulcherrima* is known to you as poinsettia. It is the various coloured bracts, be they yellow or green or red, that makes this family of plants attractive. Also they all have white sap in their stems and leaves, and when village children break off the stems of the native spurges they call the sap 'pigeons-milk'.

Festuca glauca is a neat dwarf grass of bluish tone—at 9 in. a good ground coverer. I keep mine from flowering and they are strategically placed where my dogs *will* run across a border. This is tough stuff, it is never damaged, and looks good the whole summer through.

The GENTIANA are not just Alpine flowers for the rockery. They grow well in front of the border and provide that important ingredient of blue. G. *asclepiadea* is the Willow Gentian, so called because of the shape of its leaves, and it likes its soil acid and a bit of shade. G. *gracilipes syn. purdomi* is deep blue and trailing. G. *lagodechiana* has a mid-blue trumpet in June. G. *sino-ornata* autumn flowering and 6–8 in. high; it dislikes lime and has rich blue trumpet-shaped flowers with a white stripe. It flowers from August to October, just when you need blue. Gentiana increase rapidly and can be separated and replanted each spring until you have a positive pool of blue in front of your border.

ECHINACEA is rudbeckia, the cone flower. E. *purpurea* 'Bressingham Hybrids' flower 3 ft. high from June to September—a warm rosy salmon-purple. Is there such a colour? E. 'The King' is 4 ft., flowers in August and is reddish-purple.

All GYPSOPHILAS revel in sun and a chalky soil. G. *paniculata* 'Bristol Fairy' is a very elegant form, and is 4 ft. high of baby's breath!

GALEGA is Goat's Rue, a member of the pea family—like a cultivated vetch. G. *officinalis hartlandii* 'Alba' has pure white flowers with large racemes, and grows to 5 ft.

HELIANTHUS—the sunflower. We are not talking here of the Van Gogh annual variety with those enormous heads, which are later full of seeds for the finches, but the perennials. These can also be giants: H. 'Loddon Gold' is 5 ft. with double flowers 4 in. across—August until October. H. *multiflorus* 'Capenoch Star' is a larger semi-double bright yellow anemone-flowered plant of between 5–6 ft. H. *orgyallis* (the willow sunflower) 'Monarch' has bright, deep yellow, large flowers and is 7 ft. high. Disbudding is necessary to get the largest flowers.

HELIOPSIS, which are related to the helianthus, make a good show from July onwards. They are best when they have settled in for a year: then they have a long flowering season. H. *gigantea* has large golden flowers of orange-yellow and grows to 4 ft. Its flowering season is from July to September, as is H. *scabra* 'Incomparabilis' which has zinnia-like golden-yellow flowers and is 3 ft. high. 'Light of Loddon' is free-flowering and a lighter yellow, growing to 4½ ft. 'Sonnenschild' is a really good golden-yellow at 4 ft.

The HEMEROCALLIS grows wild in America on railway banks, rather like primroses do here. It is a member of the lily family—the Day Lily—and it needs to be left in one place for a long time, preferably in front of a wall where it will grow, multiply and flourish. The Americans have gone to town with this plant and have made it very popular indeed—so popular it is almost impossible to choose from the hundreds of varieties. They grow roughly 3 ft. high and flower in profusion from June to August. There are also dwarf species. They need rich soil so, to encourage their great generosity, mulch with organic manure every spring. For those who find lilies are awkward, then here is your chance to excel. A lily that is easy and virus free. As they will stay where they are for years, make sure you free the ground of all perennial weeds before you plant. If I mention a few of the varieties available you will get an idea of the colour range. 'Apricot', 1½ ft., early June; 'Bess Vestal', maroon-red with lemon-yellow throat, 3 ft.; 'Fantasia', dull red and tan, 3 ft.; 'Gold Dust', rich orange-yellow, 3 ft.; 'Old Vintage'. wine-purple with a yellow throat, 3 ft. Gertrude Jekyll remembers the Day Lilies in her father's garden when she was a child, but it saddens one to think that they were not as glorious as they are today—but she also says they had a quantity of Musk, a delicious scent it seems they have now lost. I wonder if one day we shall wake up and run screaming to the correspondence columns of *The Times* and the gardening weeklies to say our Musk smells again! If it lost its scent so mysteriously, why should it not regain it mysteriously on some magic day to come.

You need a well-drained soil for HEUCHERA which is why perhaps I lost mine in their first season. I also put them too far back in my border—they need to be to the fore even though they are mostly 2 ft. high. The foliage is evergreen. The full range of colours (there are many named varieties, 'Pearl Drops' being white), can be obtained in the Bressingham Hybrids—which are palest pink to deepest crimson.

HOLLYHOCKS, single and double. Rust is the enemy and they must have a spot where they won't blow over. Please stake so that it does not show, with a good stake behind each spire. Hollyhocks do best in a light soil, and in towns the smoke-polluted air helps them. Why 'holly-hock' I wonder? There seems no holly about them at all. You can grow also annual hollyhocks which are dwarfish with silvery-pink flowers.

HOSTAS (plantain lilies as they used to be called) are very fashionable plants grown mostly for their foliage although I very much like the tall mauve flowers. They like moist shade, don't object to a heavy soil, and do last for years and years—but they do take a year or two to get really established. They die back completely in the winter and you really must mark where they are. Isobel Barnett, the charming TV and Radio personality, said on *Women's Hour* that she has a whole north-facing border that is nothing but hostas—partly because she loves them but secondly because she is a terribly lazy gardener (that Lady Barnett is lazy about *anything* is ridiculous and I don't believe her!) She says that once the leaves are out not a weed will grow—so that from April to October she does not have to do anything about that border at all. *H.* 'Honeybells' is scented. Sometimes the leaves are really enormous according to the season, and when properly settled in, so give them room at the initial planting. I divided some for the first time this spring, and both parents and children survived, but it is a tricky job as they are such fleshy fellows. I used a sharp trowel and was a bit drastic, but you've got to be, otherwise you will spoil all the frail crowns from which the budding leaves emerge. *H. undulata medio-variegata* is my favourite—and the slugs favourite too! This is the very wavy one you have to keep the wife away from for flower arrangements—certainly for the first year till it gets more prolific. *H. fortunei* 'Picta' is the whitest variety—off-white with greener edges to the leaves. These descriptions I'm giving you are for the leaves not the flowers! *H. sieboldiana* 'Elegans' is glorious with crinkled leaves and makes you realise where the 'plantain' name came from. *H. crispula* has white round the edges. Many nurserymen offer a collection of six different ones and this is what I bought the first time, and then ordered the ones I preferred. I also have them round a natural pond. They really are delightful there, and also under the wall facing north in my cobbled yard where their light colour is especially valuable. They are one of the few plants whose light colour is improved and intensified by shade instead of the other way round. Even the variegated hollies get greener in the shadier parts of the wood. *H. erromena* is the tallest hosta and is a plant of luxuriant beauty, with broad rich green leaves and lilac flowers on 3 ft. stems.

Iberis sempervirens 'Snowflake' is the perennial candytuft—a low-growing evergreen used in the rockery, but the dense spreading plants with their intense white flowers are useful sometimes for edging parts of the border.

IRIS. I don't think one should really waste the beauty of the iris in a mixed border, but it is valuable because of its upright sword-like leaves throughout most of the year. It needs a well-drained soil—except for *I. laevigata* and *I. sibirica* which are moisture-loving and good for the edges of ponds. *I. laevigata* will grow in shallow water. There is a very pretty variegated form I have with rich blue flowers set against beautifully variegated foliage, *I. l.* 'Variegata'. *I. pallida* 'Variegata' has blue flowers in June with grey-green leaves marked strongly with primrose-yellow, and prefers dry and sun. *I. foetidissima* 'Variegata' however, does not mind dry or deep shade. The iris does not object to a poor soil—it likes a bit of lime (so it is dangerous for a mixed border amongst acid-loving plants), and it is best planted from July to September, at a time when there is not much planting to do compared with the hectic days of spring. Irises certainly are the easiest of plants to grow and they require a minimum of attention. As I so like separate iris gardens I am going to crave the indulgence of those of you who have not room for one, and devote a whole chapter to irises later on. Those of you who would like to include irises in your borders must turn to this later chapter for the various species and varieties.

LIGULARIA are tall yellow daisy-flowered plants, which must have moisture and will flower in late summer. Worth considering are *L. clivorum* 'Desdemona' and *L. przewalskii* which has tall spires 6 ft. high of yellow. They should have plenty of space. Certainly the last named is unusual and should be included in spite of the fact it supplies yet more yellow in late summer. They need moisture in August and September when you are usually passing through a dry time, which is particularly distressing of them.

LAMIUM is useful because it will grow in the dry and will spread like all nettles. *Lamium galeobdolon* 'Variegatum' will even grow in the dry under beech trees—it has evergreen marbled leaves with spikes of soft yellow dead-nettle flowers. It is madly rampant—but who cares in dry shade where nothing else will grow! The next nettle I am fond of—it is also good for dry shade and indeed will grow anywhere—is *L. maculatum* 'Roseum'. It has clear rose-pink flowers, the leaves are sage-green striped with white and have that marvellous dead-nettle smell when you pick them. There is also *L. m.* 'Album' with pure white flowers and the leaves have a white centre. *L. m.* 'Aureum' has vivid yellow leaves marked with white but it likes moist conditions, the contrary creature. All of these do stay variegated in the shade. These dead-nettles are not used much by superior plantsmen but I, as an amateur, find them most accommodating and useful. I am not going to discard them easily.

Liatris spicata 'Kobold' has soft bottle-brush flowers of

brilliant lilac-pink above clumps of grassy foliage. It grows to about 3 ft. in height, and needs to be divided and replanted every two to three years. It is remarkable in that its flowers begin at the top of the spike in early July and then grow down the stem instead of the other way, as with most spire-shaped flowers.

Lychnis chalceodonica will flower with a head a little like a sweet william—3 ft. high and with a very bright vermilion flower. This stays flowering for a long time in June and July. There are also pink and white forms. *Lychnis viscaria* 'Splendens Plena' is a showy plant, with shocking-pink double flowers in June and July about 10 in. high. *L. coronaria* has silver foliage with the same shocking-pink single flowers, which look charming against the silver. A Fletcher favourite.

LYTHRUM, the Loosestrife family, are really for the bog-side, but still don't mind dry conditions in the border. Pink-mauve flowers are grown on erect wiry stems—long in flower. *L. salicaria* 'Prichard's variety' is rich cerise-pink, 4 ft. *L. s.* 'Fincandle' is deep rose-red.

LILIUMS—the lily. Most lilies are either easy to cultivate or difficult to grow according to the gardener. 'Surely', you retort, 'according to the soil, the situation, the feeding?' No, I'm sorry—it's the gardener! Why should lilies grow superbly well for Beverley Nichols and Edward Seago and not for the late H. E. Bates or Cyril Fletcher? Artistic, painstaking chaps, all of us! Vita Sackville-West also had troubles with lilies—admittedly the last three people mentioned lived in Kent or Sussex with clay to contend with, but one of the finest lily growers in the country is not far away and has the same sort of soil. Christopher Lloyd of Great Dixter, also on clay, says that the lilies he has greatest success with are those that produce roots from the base of the bulb only; the stem-rooters he grows in pots. The stem-rooters, he says, are more subject to slugs. Here are some very important points to make note of and inwardly digest. Good drainage is essential. Also use plenty of humus, leaf mould, peat and compost. Never use bulbs which have been out of the ground too long, and make sure their basal roots are intact. To avoid disease divide when they become overcrowded. They do not like draughts. They are best planted in the autumn. Set them on a layer of coarse sand in lime-free soil—depth varies according to variety—the stem-rooters need to have at least 6 in. of soil above them so that the roots form as the plant pushes upwards from the bulb.

Beverley Nichols writes in *Forty Favourite Flowers*—a delightful book of his I forgot to mention in an earlier chapter —that '*Lilium regale* praises the Lord'. I agree with him that it does, but it needs to have its feet amongst some lowlier shrub when doing so, as this protects the early shoots from the frost. It is a stem-rooting lily—white with a mauve tinge to it. It grows to 6 ft. in height and flowers in July with sometimes up to thirty blooms at its head. Mr Nichols grows it from seed and it flowers three years from sowing it, he says.

August is the month to plant *L. candidum*, the pure white Madonna Lily which flowers in June and July; it likes lime, roots from the base, is sometimes evergreen. These lilies need to be planted only an inch deep, or even less, with their noses nearly showing. *L. auratum* is a stem-rooter, likes the soil lime-free, and to be 8 in. deep. The flowers, basically white with crimson markings on yellow stripes, are enormous on 6 ft. stems in August. *L. chalcedonicum* is the Orange Lily—the symbol of the Orangemen in Northern Ireland. This does well in a stiff soil even though it is a stem-rooter, and needs to be planted 5 in. deep. The martagon or Turk's Cap Lily, has slender spikes of pinkish-purpleish flowers spotted purple-black and looking down, if you get my meaning. Base rooting, June/July. The Tiger Lily, *L. tigrinum*, used to be grown by the Japanese as a food. It likes a richly manured soil—hates lime—is stem-rooting and needs to be planted 8 in. deep. *L. pardalinum* is the Panther lily of California and Oregon, and is one of the hardiest and easiest. It likes part shade, is base-rooting and produces large open clusters of orange-red flowers spotted with purple from July to August on 6–8 ft. stems. I think I have mentioned enough lilies for beginners, so let us hope you will be among the successful growers. I am going to start again with lilies in my new midden garden. I cannot imagine anything more beautiful against my old stone grey walls.

MONARDA is bergamot, an old herb the Elizabethans knew. It grows 3–4 ft. high. *M.* 'Cambridge Scarlet' is the popular one and will provide a mound of bright scarlet in July. *M.* 'Prairie Night' is purple, but let's have the scarlet.

Nepeta mussinii—the catmint. My black cat, who is a quarter Siamese, loves eating my nepeta and as I have the 2 ft. variety *N.* 'Six Hills' there is plenty of it for him. It must be a tonic for cats, for he is a very hale and hearty twenty-one-year-old as I write. Both his brothers lived to be fifteen. Nepeta is inclined to die in the winter if it is left in the damp. I don't take the dead leaves and flowers off mine in the autumn clear-up, and this helps survival I think. *N. grandiflora* 'Blue Beauty' has erect spikes of lavender-blue, 1½ ft. high. If you keep the blooms cut as they fade, then you will get a succession of blooms all summer, but do not move it or divide it in the autumn or winter; if you do it will die.

The Evening Primrose or OENOTHERA one used to see in Wiltshire at the side of the road on rubbish heaps when I was a boy, but it has become a more sophisticated plant today. *O.* 'Fireworks' is excellent for the front of the border, has red buds and yellow flowers, from June to August, and is 1½ ft. high. *O. glauca* has shiny grey-green foliage, is 2 ft. high, and flowers June to September. They must have plenty of sun. *O. speciosa* 'Rosea' is dwarf (1 ft.), and has flowers which open pink and die off a deeper shade.

The POM-POM CHRYSANTHEMUM is an invaluable late season flower for the border. It is sturdy and needs no staking. I have little groups of them in the front of the border. Also useful are the KOREAN CHRYSANTHEMUMS, *C. koreanum*, with thin single, double and semi-double flowers. They are hardy, and divide easily. Their colours range from soft pink to rust-bronze and wine-red, and canary-yellow and white. You can propagate from cuttings in March which will root in the cool greenhouse.

Solomon's Seal—POLYGONATUM—is a shade-lover with arching stems and bells of greenish-white, but you must not let it dry out. *P. multiflorum* is the old garden favourite.

Fancy cultivating members of the dock family? I do, and I hope you will. *Polygonum bistorta* 'Superbum' has leaves very like a dock, and in May large pink flowers on tall 3 ft. stems—then when the first flush is over it will send up shorter-stemmed smaller flowers right on into the autumn. Divide only in the spring. *P. affine* is for rock gardens and paths. Rich crimson spikes like lavender come from *P. atrosanguineum* from June to autumn.

I don't think I mentioned ANTHEMIS 'Thora Perry' earlier on—she is a creamy-yellow daisy with fern-like foliage which blooms from June to August, a long period. At points of the border away from her, also in groups of four or five plants a time, do try the anthemis 'Perry's variety'; another yellow variety is 'E. C. Buxton'. These are old-fashioned plants, and I have been growing them with delight for thirty-five years. A whole lot of the catalogues don't seem to have them and none of the writers—except the older ones like Eleanor Sinclair Rhode—seem to mention them—and I nearly left them out!

PENTSTEMON used to be treated rather as one does the pelargonium—out of the cool greenhouse or frame into the garden for the summer and then back again. In my garden at East Grinstead thirty years ago, there were a lot of these, sometimes too many to get back into the frames—and some which had got themselves into the kitchen gardens and amongst the fruit. I used to leave them to the worst the frost could do to them—and they were not the new hardy strains—but they even survived the awful winter of 1947, or most of them did. In a way pentstemons look like a snapdragon with a foxglove flower. There is a demureness about them as they look down. They need full sun, and flower from June to August. *P. gloxinoides* is the common garden kind; *P. hartwegii* and *P.* 'Newbury Gem' are a fine scarlet. There is one called 'Ruby' which should have been called 'Magenta'! *P. h.* 'Garnet' is red again, with more delicate flowers, and *P. digitaloides* bears out my claim that it looks like a foxglove. A new hybrid, *P. fruticosus* 'Katherine de la Mer', is lilac-pink and hardy.

PHYSOSTEGIA are easy to grow, and different kinds flower from June to September. It spreads rapidly. *P. virginia* 'Bouquet Rose' is a late-flowering deep pink 2½ ft. high, and *P. v.* 'Summer Snow' is white in the autumn. Physostegias are known as the Obedient Plants because they have hinged stalks and will stay where they are put!

As well as the shrub POTENTILLA, there are the plants which also flower for prodigously long periods. They have strawberry-type leaves, some of them silvery. *P. flammea* has large flowers of intense crimson-red. *P.* 'Gibson's Scarlet' has maroon centres to scarlet flowers. *P.* 'William Rollison' has double orange-yellow flowers. They look rather like geums and my gardener insists they are geums no matter how I argue with him. He always will think they are geums too!

PULMONARIA is the Lungwort. It grows wild in Sussex where it is called Soldiers-Sailors, for the flowers are pink and blue. It flowers from March to May. *P. rubra* will flower soon after Christmas and is 9 in. high. *P. azurea* is 10 in. high and flowers the same time as the forsythia—so put some round the base of your bushes.

SALVIA is of the sage family. I do have the variegated sage in my border. *S. supurba* has many erect spikes of violet-blue 3–4 ft. from June to August, and if you cut them back they will come again. *S. lubeca* is a dwarf form, very rich in colour.

The SEDUMS are ardent sun lovers and will bring as many butterflies to your garden as the buddleias do. *Sedum* 'Autumn

Joy' has large flat-headed flowers of rich salmon-bronze about 18 in. high. *S.* 'Ruby Glow' is 9 in. high, and forms a spreading mat of red just when you need it, from August until October. *S. spectabile* 'Brilliant' is a glorious plant, about 1 ft. in height, and makes a dense clump of magenta-pink flowers.

SIDALCEAS belong to the mallow family, and when I tell you that I had my first ones as a wedding present thirty-two years ago and I have moved some of them with me to and from four different gardens, you will realise they are fairly easy plants. *S.* 'Sussex Beauty' is pink and comes in June for many weeks, 3 ft. tall. The ones I moved so much were *S.* 'Rosy Gem', *S.* 'Rose Queen' and *S.* 'Interlaken', though I have lost track by now of the ones that have survived.

Senecio przewalskii 'The Rocket' has a quaintness which should be included in all borders as a talking point. It has 6 ft. high black stems for a start! It likes a rich moist soil and flowers in June/July with spires of yellow tiny daisy-like flowers.

Tradescantia rubra has purple-red three-petalled flowers in short rush-like leaves. *T.* 'Purple Dome' is purple. They are all about 1 ft. high, they flower for a long time and are hardy. *T.* 'Osprey' is pure white, *T.* 'Isis' is a deep blue.

Veronica incana has spikes of intense blue flowers 1 ft. high on mats of silvery-blue leaves. *V. teucrium* 'Crater Lake Blue' is an intense dark blue in June and July. *V. virginica* 'Alba' is 5 ft. high with thin graceful spikes of white, and does not need staking.

ZANTEDESCHIA 'Crowborough Variety' is an Arum Lily which grows freely in the open here in Sussex, but they need to be covered with straw or litter in more northerly climes. If you do not want to risk it in the open border you can sink it a foot deep in the pond and it will not be affected by the frost at all.

Well if you have all that lot you will have a wonderful border or bed. My first herbaceous border had one hundred and twenty different varieties in it, with over six hundred and fifty separate plants all mapped out in a plan. I was twenty-eight years old at the time, and my mother-in-law, who was over sixty, helped me plant it. She put in many more of the plants than I did and every one of them lived. The border that next summer was a picture—it needed to be, it was 1942 and we deserved a tonic. In my mind's eye I can still see it, and enjoy it. Looking at the plan and the list of plants I have kept in my gardening note book, I can remember each plant. It is a very valuable adjunct to any gardener—a note book. Mine is a green leather volume given me by my wife the first year of our marriage. It is divided into separate compartments with a tab at the beginning of each: bulbs, seeds, annuals, perennials, rock plants, roses, trees and shrubs, fruit trees, vegetables, sundries, and two blanks which I have not yet found the need for. Oh, if only I entered more in it! One finds a particular variety which is especially pleasing, but over the years one forgets it. If you write down its name—there it is thirty-three years later.

12 Grey-leaved and Foliage Plants

First of all, dear reader, let me tell you of two standard works which must be useful: *Grey and Silver Plants* published by Collins, and written by Mrs Desmond Underwood. Those of you who go to the Chelsea Show will know of the magnificent exhibit staged by Mrs Underwood each year and thronged to so eagerly by the public. Here are all the grey plants in their glory. The second book is from the same publisher, *Foliage Plants* by Christopher Lloyd, who owns a garden at Great Dixter.

Mr Lloyd claims that 'Appreciation of foliage comes at a late stage in our education if it comes at all', and goes on to say that it is an acquired taste.

He is right. But we do get more sophisticated and more knowledgeable these days more quickly. There are more books about gardening, every daily paper carries most excellent and erudite articles, and we are given splendid programmes on radio and television. So I am sure there is a great number of amateur gardeners who realise the value of foliage. Today with such a rich cult in flower arranging, many gardeners know that foliage is just as important as the flowers.

The grey foliage plants come to mind first. They all love the sun. Indeed sun is essential to the plant otherwise it does not have its silvery appearance. This silvery look is given by white and silver hairs which are produced by the plant as a protection against the drying effects of the sun. The bloom on the glaucous foliage of the pink and carnation family (*dianthus*) is similarly caused.

Many of the grey-leaved plants originate in the Mediterranean regions, so they are immediately thought of as half-hardy. But in Corsica, Sardinia and indeed Italy and the south of France, a lot of these grow at a considerable altitude in their native lands. What is essential is that they should all be in the sun so that the new wood, as it were, is well matured by the autumn, and that they should always be on a well-drained site. It is not so much a cold wind or a sharp frost but a soggy soil round the base of the plant that will rot it. Mrs Underwood goes to great lengths in her catalogue of grey foliage plants to classify her plants as to their hardiness in certain soils and certain areas. Like most women she is more painstaking than the mere male. There are some wet winters, however, followed by very cold springs, in which losses are bound to occur. Here again, a little ingenuity and care, once we are alerted to the dangers, will mitigate many a tragedy. Do not be too dismayed, then, if you are on heavy clay soil; it is reasonably easy to give your plants the extra drainage they will require. If the base of the plant is raised above the level of the surrounding ground it helps. If you put a lot of these plants in on the top of a dry retaining wall, they will prosper. A clever expedient suggested by Mrs Underwood is to pot the precious plant in a 6 in. pot, knock out the botton of the pot, and then plunge it half-way into the border.

The grey plants do not prefer an acid soil but will tolerate it—most of them coming from limestone areas. Coastal areas are ideal for grey-leaved plants. Urban gardens, because of the polluted air, are not as good for grey-foliaged plants as the open countryside.

The shape of all shrubs and plants is important, but when you are planting a shrub for its leaves then it is *all*-important. If a shrub should arrive from the nursery all lop-sided because one side of it has been drawn to the sun, do not be tempted to plant it this way round to continue its deformity. Plant it the other way so that its sparse side will flourish in the sun and the whole become balanced. Also make sure leggy specimens are 'stopped' at frequent intervals so that the shrub is compact. Pruning for grey-leaved shrubs is usually in the spring, and it is necessary to dead-head all of them. Remember that you do not want to encourage any new shoots late in the season—it is these tender shoots which will be spoilt by the frost and rotting will set in. We only want sun-hardened mature shoots for the winter to wreak its havoc on.

A completely grey border is not a good idea in this country when skies are so infrequently blue. A grey and white border planted by a genius like the late Vita Sackville-West is a glory to behold. Generally you should use the greys and silvers to show off other plants. They associate most beautifully with pinks, blues or mauves. They are a tremendous help in a garden to split up two pinks, or two reds, or two oranges which to-gether might shout terribly at each other, but with a good blob of silver in between, will even enhance each other. As a small boy I thought the word 'enhance' was spelled and pronounced as 'enchance', as if it were part of 'enchanted'. Somehow it still seems to me that this word should be included in the English dictionary.

Acaena ascendens comes from New Zealand and is useful for trailing over walls and banks and intermingling with and through other plants which become uninteresting after their flowering season. There is a robust cultivar called 'Blue Haze' which is richly glaucous and spreads.

ACHILLEA. There are several silver ones—all have the delicate filigree foliage, fernlike and beautiful. *A.* 'Argentea' is for the rockery or edging and has tiny rosettes of silver white leaves and white flowers in June. *A.* 'Kolbiana' forms a cushion of scented foliage and white flowers (grey and with scented foliage, it's bound to be a favourite with me). *A.* 'Moonshine' is a lovely plant grown to great effect at Great Dixter with grey fern-like foliage and yellow flowers 2 ft. tall.

ANAPHALIS I have mentioned before with the herbaceous border plants, and I would not be without it. It is distinctly silver-grey. It is no bother, spreads, but not too much, has everlasting flowers for drying and does not need staking. The greyest one *A. triplinervis* which has larger, bolder leaves, and *A. nubigena* (about 8 in.), flower in August.

Anthemis cupiana is a robust mat-former, whose merits I have sung already, especially the fragrance of its finely dissected grey foliage after rain. Its white daisy flowers need to be cut after flowering, otherwise they go black and the whole plant looks untidy. You will get more flowers later on then. It is very invasive and you will give it lots of liberties. One that I allow is *A. cupaniana*, invading the ground under six bushes of Hybrid Tea 'Papa Meilland'—the dark claret rose which smells as all roses should. The rose does not like this at all but the grey lightens the background for the dark red, and it glows. *Anthemis rudolphiana* is a 6 in. edging with a feathery silvery leaf.

ARTEMESIA form a large group of herbaceous plants and sub-shrubs, most of them grey and all of them with feathery-lacy plumage instead of leaves! *A. absinthium* is the well-known 'Lambrook Silver'—it forms hummocks of silvery, feathery, fan-shaped leaves about 18 in. high, with plumes of flowers 3 ft. high which, when you first own the plant, persuade you that they are going to bloom into something quite spectacular. It never does bloom and you have these bud-like flowers rather similar to lead shot. Do not let these sprays of lead shot stay too long on the plant as they eventually turn to a rather yellow-ish-grey which is unattractive. *A. aborescens* is really a shrub and is only half-hardy—shimmering silver at 3–4 ft. high, it needs very good drainage and is excellent if it is backed by a wall, thus standing a better chance. *A. discolor* is also a fine and feathery shrub only 18 in. tall, but extremely hardy. *A. glacialis* is for the rockery. *A. lanata* 'Pedemontana' is only 6 in. tall, is very shrubby, spreads quickly and looks well in winter. Palest, brightest silvery-grey and 3 ft. in height is *A. ludoviciana*. For those with clay soil and who are not ad-venturous, *A. nutans* has fine lacy foliage. *A. abrotanum* is Old Man's Beard, or Lad's Love (according to your age) and is known by most as Southernwood. It grows happily on my clay—but it is greenish-grey and the foliage very pleasantly aromatic. It is most definitely a shrub and needs to be kept to about 3 ft. high and then it will broaden into a cloud of lacy foliage.

Atriplex halimus is an evergreen, silvery shrub 4 ft. high. *A. hortensis* is quite different, looks like purple spinach—and you can eat it!

CENTAUREA is the old fashioned cornflower family. *C. gymnocarpa* is, in the opinion of Mr Christopher Lloyd, the most beautiful of all grey leaves. Alas, *C. gymnocarpa* cannot be relied upon for hardiness, and you must take cuttings each September for a cold frame. It has finely-cut grey leaves and thistle-like—perhaps Knapweed-like is a closer description—flowers of mauve. These flowers are not very handsome and should be removed. 2½ ft. high.

Convolvulus creorum. When I first saw this plant I just could not believe its beauty. I just could not credit the silveryness of its leaves—and then the glory of its pink, but only just, flushed white flowers. It is a difficult plant. I can't manage it on my clay, or perhaps it would be best to say I have not the time to cosset it on my clay. It is 2 ft. high of sheer glory.

Eucalyptus gunnii grows very quickly indeed. A foot high shrublet can be a 20 ft. tree in three years. Like all eucalyptus it has mature foliage and juvenile foliage; you need to keep the trees constantly trimmed, for it is the immature foliage that you need for very long lasting flower decorations. The eucalyptus is not hardy but it is cheap and, growing quickly, replaceable. If you are fortunate, you will buy one grown either from native English seed or Australian seed, which has come from a high altitude where the seed's parents are used to a colder climate. *E. perriniana* has juvenile leaves threaded on its branches like kebab. *E. niphophila* is a smallish tree when mature, and very glaucous.

Euphorbia myrsinites has blue-grey foliage, but in the spring the flowers and bracts are lime-green, as in all euphorbias.

Festuca glauca is the Blue Grass. This is only 6 in. high and can be used effectively for edging. It is an admirable plant to use if you have a place in your garden which is used as a path by your dogs and you wish they did not. They will, of course, so you might just as well put something there which looks decorative but will come to no harm. *Festuca glauca* is just the thing. I do not like mine to flower, they look spindly, but they keep their freshness if you cut off their flower spikes.

Several of the HEBES are glaucous rather than silvery. *Hebe bageana* is dark blue-grey.

Do not forget the grey mint, 'Bowle's Variety', which as well as grey-felted leaves, blooms pleasantly mauve.

Helichrysum angustifolium has bright silvery foliage; it makes a bushy shrub, and has rather undistinguished yellow flowers—these, if left on the plant, become a goldish-brown, a very dingy colour which remains for a long time and takes all the pleasure from the plant. Do cut them off. Trim the shrub, too, for new silvery foliage, but not later than August.

Helichrysum petiolatum has a spreading habit and is charming with its white felted leaves, but it is not hardy with me—even planted in a well-drained tub. Take your cuttings in the autumn and keep in a greenhouse away from frost but not in a hot-house atmosphere. It is lovely with pelargoniums in a tub or ornamental vase.

Lavendula—I have rhapsodised already on all the lavenders—the whitest, or silveriest of which are the Dutch Lavenders, 2 ft. high. There is a white lavender, too, which by having white flowers makes the leaves seem more silvery.

Onopordon arabicum—can be a nightmare thistle growing 8 ft. high—but it is shining silver. If you want this biennial to stay with you, just cut it back and do not let it flower. To my mind this is sacrilege and spoils the look of the noble giant—besides, the flowers are fun! Once you have a few of these in the garden and allow them to flower, you will always find the odd seedling here and there, not enough to be a nuisance though. This plant is perfectly hardy and can be grown most easily from seed. If you start the seed off early in the greenhouse it will flower the same year. Do give it plenty of room; if well placed it will not need staking, and if you do have to stake it, it will look awkward.

Salvia argentea has large white-felted leaves which are especially memorable if you see them with dew on them in the early September sun. Slugs adore them. They need looking after on damp ground but they are well worth the trouble. These, too, are biennial—but I let mine flower, and so long as I do not let them seed, the plants seem to grow happily year after year.

Santolina chamaecyparissus 'Incana' is the Cotton Lavender I am so fond of, and have mentioned several times; *S. c.* 'Nana' is a dwarf variety. *S. c.* 'Weston' is the whitest and woolliest. Do not let it flower. The flowers are miserable little yellow balls with an offensive smell, which when they die, stay on the plant a long time and spoil the look of it. Keep the mound-like bushes pruned well—actually if you are married to a flower arranger this will be done for you, for there is no more useful plant to help an arrangement 'stay up'—or to enhance the colours you are using.

Of moderate hardiness is *Senecio cineraria* but it has survived the last three winters very easily with me in Sussex. There are two kinds which I particularly like: *S. c.* 'White Diamond'—the whitest of them all—and *S. c.* 'Ramparts' which has felted leaves with more deeply cut foliage. *S. leucostachys* is too frail a plant to my mind, and it looks anaemic. *S. greyi* is a low-growing shrub with silvery-grey—almost white—on the undersides, evergreen leaves, and yellow flowers in June and July. It comes from New Zealand and is hardy. It will grow very easily from cuttings.

There are two kinds of *Stachys lanata* (Lamb's Lugs or Rabbit's Ears), the usual one with flowers 18 in. tall of pink which fade and are woody and unsightly, but very beautiful as buds—and the *S. l.* 'Silver Carpet' which does not flower.

Verbascum bombyciferum is a silver-felted plant with large leaves and a 4 ft. spike of yellow. It is a biennial, so if it is allowed to flower it will die the same year. If you stop it flowering each year you will just have a large clump of spectacular silver leaves. I love the flowers and think it is worth the bother of sowing fresh seed every year. The yellow spires are very striking and the yellow looks so well with the white, felted leaves.

There are grey-blues amongst the conifers. Indeed, one might say there are silver conifers but please refer to the chapter on conifers to avoid repetition.

I headed this chapter *Grey-Leaved and Foliage Plants*. We have listed the principal popular greys here. There are other unusual colours like purple and blue and then the yellows and variegated plants.

I have mentioned so many purple plants in my shrubbery chapter that I dare not repeat them all again but here is a brief list:

Acer palmatum 'Dissectum Atropurpureum
Acer palmatum 'Linearilobum Purpureum'
Berberis thunbergii 'Atropurpurea'
Berberis thunbergii 'Atropurpurea Nana'
Berberis thunbergii 'Rose Glow'
Corylopsis willmottiae 'Spring Purple
Corylus maxima 'Purpurea'
Cotinus coggygria 'Royal Purple'
Cotinus coggygria 'Rubrifolius'
Euonymus europaeus 'Atropurpureus'
Phormium tenex 'Purpureum'
Prunus spinosa 'Purpurea'
Weigela florida 'Foliis Purpureis'.

The placing of them is important. I have just returned from an exciting morning at Dartington Hall in Totnes in Devonshire. The views and the shape and the vistas and the use of various levels in this garden are thrilling. But the planting compared to the planting at Sheffield Park or in smaller gardens at Dixter and Sissinghurst is most disappointing. In one instance there are several lovely bushes of what was known as *Rhus cotinus*, and is now *Cotinus coggygria* 'Royal Purple', right slap-bang in front of a *Pissardii nigra*—the purple-flowering Plum. Surely it needed a backing of grey or green with white variegation or blue? There were far too many junipers of the *pfitzerana* kind—such a great monotony of planting all over the gardens, as if the plants had come in job lots of so many dozen at the time, but how magnificent the trees and the vast lawns and the tiltyard and the steps!

Who am I to criticise in my humble way with my own particular mistakes sticking out a mile! This brings me to a useful thought. Try during each season to go round your plot with a pencil and pad and re-arrange on paper what you would do to eliminate your planting mistakes. Assemble your notes in the autumn and then amend what you can. Do not be too daring with very well-established trees, large shrubs or items like magnolias which hate to be moved—rather dislike their position than lose an old friend.

The variegated shrubs one can choose from are:

Abutilon megapotamicum 'Variegatum'
Abutilon × *milleri*
Acer palmatum: several cvs., especially:
    A.p. 'Albomarginatum'
    A.p. 'Dissectum Variegatum
Aralia elata 'Aureovariegata'
    A.e. 'Variegata'
Aucuba japonica: several cvs., especially:
    A.j. 'Crotonifolia'
    A.j. 'Gold Dust'
Azara microphylla 'Variegata'
Berberis thunbergii 'Rose Glow'
Buddleia daviddii 'Harlequin'
Buxus sempervirens 'Elegantissima'
Cornus alba 'Elegantissima'
    C.a. 'Spaethii'
    C.a. 'Variegata'
Cornus alternifolia 'Argentea
Cornus mas 'Variegata'
Cotoneaster horizontalis 'Variegata'
Crataegus oxyzacantha, 'Gireoudii'
Daphne odora 'Aureomarginata'
Elaeagnus pungens
Euonymus fortunei 'Silver Queen'
    E.f. 'Variegatus'
Euonymus japonica
Fatsia japonica 'Variegata'
Fuchsia magellanica 'Variegata'
    F.m. 'Versicolor'
Hebe × *andersonii* 'Variegata'
Hebe × *franciscana* 'Variegata'
Hebe glaucophylla 'Variegata'
Hibiscus syriacus 'Meehanii'
Hydrangea macrophylla 'Maculata'
    H.m. 'Tricolor'
Hypericum × *moseranum* 'Tricolor'

Ilex aquifolium 'Argenteomarginata'
    I.a. 'Aureomarginata'
    I.a. 'Golden Milkboy'
    I.a. 'Grandis'
    I.a. 'Handsworth New Silver'
    I.a. 'Ovata Aurea'
Kerria japonica 'Variegata'
Ligustrum sinense 'Variegatum'
Myrtus communis 'Variegatus'
Osmanthus heterophyllus 'Aureomarginatus'
    O.m. 'Latifolius Variegatus'
    O.m. 'Variegatus'
Pachysandra terminalis 'Variegata'
Philadelphus coronarius 'Variegatus'
Pieris japonica 'Variegata'
Pittosporum eugenioides 'Variegatum'
Pittosporum tenuifolium, several cvs., including:
    P.t. 'Silver Queen'
    P.t. 'Variegatum'
Prunus laurocerasus 'Variegata'
Prunus lusitanica 'Variegata'
Rhododendron ponticum 'Variegatum
Rubus microphyllus 'Variegatus'
Ruta graveolens 'Variegata'
Salvia officianalis 'Icterina'
    S.o. 'Tricolor'
Sambucus nigra 'Albovariegata'
    S.n. 'Aureomarginata'
    S.n. 'Pulverulenta'
Syringa emodii 'Aureovariegata'
Viburnum tinus 'Variegata'
Vinca major 'Maculata'
    V.m. 'Variegata'
Vinca minor 'Variegata'
Weigela florida 'Variegata'
Weigela praecox 'Variegata'

Amongst the giants is *Gunnera manicata*. This, for some people, my daughter included, is quite a frightening plant, so if you only appreciate the minute and do not want to walk under giant leaves of hairy rhubarb, ignore the *Gunnera*. If you like imposing plants, the *Acanthus spinosus* can reach 6 ft. Its finely cut leaves are the inspiration for the designs on Greek columns and on Georgian houses and furniture. In a way similar to the acanthus is the cardoon *Cynara cardunculus* which is the most decorative but inedible form of the globe artichoke *Cynara scolymus* which is, to my mind, just as beautiful—but do not cut them all for eating; let us see some of those magnificent purple thistle heads.

Whilst thinking of height and the unusual, there are the grasses to consider. *Miscanthus sinensis* 'Zebrinus' is a tall grass growing to 5 ft.—with a magnificent fountain of green with yellowish bands going across the width of the grass, but not along the length of it, as has *Miscanthus sinensis* 'Variegatus'. It is also shorter. I have a 'hedge' of these two varieties planted alternately and it is one of my happier inspirations. I needed some shelter on a windy site for some new hedge cupressus I had planted, and on the windward side the grasses look magnificent. I shall leave them there even when the hedge is taller than they are. In spring and early summer (late in the season, too, if you are busy with your shears on both foliage and seed heads as soon as the seed head is fully grown) a very pretty grass is *Phalaris arundinacea* 'Picta'. It was a most familiar plant in Victorian gardens and cottage gardens, and is too valuable to ignore. It is green and yellow and parchment-white in stripes and it colonises quickly and vigorously. I bought one little plant from a W.V.S. stall in Lewes market six years ago. I have thrown barrowloads of it away, given it away and used it to colonise a dry clay-baked border at the side of my drive. This it has done effectively—daffodils come through first, a thick covering of a couple of thousand, and then the grass comes to hide the daffodil foliage as it dies—that is the theory which doesn't quite work, but I am going to have another look at it next spring! This plant is also known as Gardener's Garters, and it grows in a pond if you like it that way. *M. sacchariflorus* is the tallest of the ornamental grasses and grows to 10 ft. or so with me on my wealden clay soil.

It is a short step visually from grasses to the bamboos, and here is a treasury of remarkable foliage plants. Most bamboos spread inordinately—because of this, for some folk the bamboo is taboo. Others do not mind using a spade to keep the clump the same size at the end of the season. It is often used effectively in the mixed border—well to the back, of course, or on an island site as the pivotal plant. They are excellent as specimen plants in small courtyards or cobbled yards. Sometimes they look sick in winter when some of the leaves not only turn khaki but get torn and still stay forlornly on the plant. It is best to plant them in the late spring in warm, damp ground. They do not like moving and may take a year to recover. *Arundinaria murielae* is a slender elegant soft green, 8–12 ft. high. *A. vagans* is dwarf and a creeper and a stifler. *Phyllostachys nigra* grows to 10 ft. with black stems. *P. viridi-glaucescens* is for the large garden, growing to 18 ft. or more with yellow-green canes, purple at the joints. Give all bamboos a soil rich in humus and some shade.

Among the variegated plants, let me remind you of the dead-nettles (*L. galeobdolon* 'Variegatum'), the apple mint (*M. rotundifolia* 'Variegata'), which is only 12 in. tall and has green leaves with large white splodges, and the variegated sage, *Salvia officinalis* which is cream, pink and purple with grey and green thrown in for good measure. There is also a purple sage, *Salvia officinalis* 'Purpurascens' to add to your purple-leaved plants. The Common Bugle which has little spires of dark blue and deep plum-coloured foliage will rush and tumble about the whole garden if you let it. It is a useful plant though, and I would not be without it. I do not believe in depriving myself of a plant because it is too easy. This is the plant I dote on. There is also a deep copper-purple four-leaved clover which romps away but which is very beautiful. Have we mentioned the variegated vincas? They will overrun you but not the first two years or so; they need to establish themselves. Also remember that some of the heathers have foliage which is richly coloured.

13 Odd Odours

Read what one of our earlier gardeners says about aromatic plants. Francis Bacon in his *Essays* writes:

'And because the breath of flowers if far sweeter in the air (where it comes and goes like the warbling of music) than in the hand, therefore nothing is more fit for that delight, than to know what be the flowers and plants that do best perfume the air. Roses, damask and red, are fast flowers of their smells; so that you may walk by a whole row of them, and find nothing of their sweetness; yea though it be in a morning's dew. Bays likewise yield no smell as they grow. Rosemary little; nor sweet marjoram. That which above all others yields the sweetest smell in the air, is the violet, especially the white double violet which comes twice a year; about the middle of April, and about bartholomew-tide. Next to that is the musk-rose. Then the strawberry-leaves dying, with a most excellent cordial smell. Then the flower of the vines; it is a little dust, like the dust of a bent, which grows upon the cluster in the first coming forth. Then sweet-briar. Then wall-flowers which are very delightful to be set under a parlour or lower chamber window. Then pinks and gilliflowers, specially the matted pink and clove gilliflower. Then the flowers of the lime-tree. Then the honeysuckles, so they be somewhat afar off. Of bean-flowers I speak not, because they are field flowers. But those which perfume the air most delightfully, not passed by as the rest, but being trodden upon and crushed, are three; that is, burnet, wild-thyme, and watermints. Therefore you are to set whole alleys of them, to have the pleasure when you walk or tread.'

But to get back to the title of our chapter. By this, I do NOT mean a chap who recites funny poems. Those of you who follow my *Gardening Today* television programmes from the Midlands will know how keen I am on natural manures—well,

I don't mean that sort of pong either. I write of the aromatic plants, not necessarily with the perfume coming from the blooms, but plants which give off a sometimes subtle and sometimes pungent aroma. These aromatic plants come largely from Mediterranean regions and are accustomed to basking in sunshine—and it is this fierce sunshine that brings out the heady perfume. The aroma comes from the volatile oils within the plant. This volatile oil is called by some gardeners—what a picturesque word—ethereal. So, as you wander round your garden, you breathe in the ethereal perfume.

It is one of my favourite pastimes to take friends round my garden and to give them a leaf to rub in the hands, of this plant and of that, and get them to guess what it is or perhaps what the particular aroma is. You must make two kinds of excursions, either in the full sun as Wordsworth's Waggoner had it, when: 'The air as in a lion's den is close and hot', or on a wet day, dewy morning or still evening.

Let us take the first excursion on a blazing summer's day. Like the scent from an old cedar box comes the hot laden air from the cypress, especially the common Lawson's. How rewarding it is to work under a hedge of it on a summer's noon! It helps to give you your first thirst. Somewhat similar is the scent given off from the sticky leaves of the giant rock roses *Cistus ladaniferus* (that is to say 'yielding ladanum', a gum). Rub your fingers lightly over the leaves for a lasting effect. There is also *Cistus laurifolium* with dark sticky leaves. This has large, white papery flowers which only last for a day, but so bountiful a shrub is she that the flowering season is a long one.

The most lasting effect of any aroma in your garden will come from the silver leaves of the curry plant. This isn't the plant that curry flavour comes from, but it outshines Mike Yarwood in its impression and it is called *Helichrysum angustifolium*. You had better visit this one last of all on your itinerary as its flavour on the fingers is so very strong and lingering. Early in the summer, when its buds are bursting and its leaves are still sticky— no need to feel a leaf here, you will get it strongly in the breeze and heady it is too—comes the fragrance of a balsam poplar (so redolent of spring and early summer). The tree grows quickly and will fill your garden with scent. What grows quicker, though, than *Eucalyptus gunnii*? You will need to crush the leaf here, but not with *Eucalyptus citriodora* with its citron-scented leaves. Lemon-scented, too, is *Melissa Officinalis* 'Aurea', a brightly golden-leaved, scented balm.

Cotton lavender has a slightly lemon scent combined, and

this seems a contradiction, with a pleasant 'paraffiny' smell. This scent is lingering and my English Setter, Samantha, lies on an enormous bush of it on the terrace in the sun and her head smells of it when she rests it on my knee. The other lavenders are too well known to mention, but remember the dwarf kinds if your garden is small. Rosemary is a sweet scent and is useful for garnishing roast lamb but do remember, chaps, to keep the bush a reasonable size. It is said that if the rosemary grows over-strongly in the garden then the wife is the one who wears the trousers (Silly, out-of-date plant—they all do!)

Then there is sage. I should prefer the variegated variety and there is no prettier small plant for a wall or rockery than variegated thyme. There is a lemon-scented thyme as well. *Rhododendron glaucophyllum* has greyish leaves—the undersides white with bell-shaped flowers of old rose—and this bush is gloriously aromatic. *R. g.* 'Luteiflorum', from Burma, has lemon-yellow flowers.

On your evening walk, or perhaps your early-morning dewy walk, or your summer-day walk in the rain, you notice how box seems to give off its pleasant olde-worlde scent best in the damp. *Anthemis cupaniana* with its large mats of silver-grey foliage has a glorious aroma all through the year when wet, but its white flowers smell, to my mind, rather unpleasantly, especially in the house. The sweet briar rose is best when wet. I have them placed at strategic points all over the garden—I would not be without it. My grandmother used to crush a leaf when we were children and stuff it down the inside of our collars and when we undressed at night we would find the crushed and rather prickly leaf, still aromatic, in our singlets.

The mints—the ordinary garden mint and the Eau-de-Cologne mint (such a vigorous and invasive fellow) are good in the evening. Another aromatic herb is the bergamot, or mon-arda, much loved by the Elizabethans, though left out by Mr Bacon. Indeed the ethereal oil from the bergamot orange (*citrus borgamia*)—is used for making Eau-de-Cologne and is French. Can we grow it here, I wonder, as we grow the other bergamots? (I've never been able to buy one to try it).

And when you get your friend back into the house you can entertain him with the various charms of the scented pelar-goniums—mint, lemon, rose, nutmeg, balsam and peppermint. What a galaxy! And what better incense than that ascending heavenwards when a thin column of blue wood-smoke rises on a frosty winter's morning from a snug fireside.

14 The Water Garden

A pond is an aesthetically beautiful addition to the garden, be it a formal pond 2 ft. square or a lake of several acres—it provides another element, another dimension and a complete change of scene. It is an added ornament to the whole garden. It is these days an easily added ornament because of such modern substances as fibre glass and plastic sheeting. Many years ago it was an expensive item to add a fountain to your pool; for this needed connection to the main water supply, but today this lovely addition is simply supplied by an electric pump.

For the lazy gardener a large area of water is a necessity. It will never have to be dug, mown, pruned or weeded—indeed the most you can do with a pond is to lie beside it in a deck chair and appreciate its wonderfully relaxing properties and study the natural history of the aquatic life—a most rewarding occupation.

There are three kinds of water gardens: the formal pool, the natural pond and lake, and the riverside garden. The formal pool is usually of a geometric shape which is part of a formal garden, perhaps sunken on a terrace, and is usually edged by paving, or stone of some kind. The natural pond or lake is frequently indigenous but is quite easily made, its edges planted with aquatic or swamp plants and shrubs and grasses. The riverside garden is more rare and needs a special approach. I would like to recommend an excellent book: *Riverside Gardening* by Mary Chaplin, published by Collingridge. This well-illustrated book explains in detail that planning of gardens on banks of canals, rivers or streams, where there is movement of water, is not as simple as it seems at first. It deals with flooding, erosion and the protection and planting of banks. This is a large and specialised subject and not, I think, to be discussed in detail here in my book, although I did live in a water-mill for three years and I will give the odd hint or two.

The formal pool is the simplest of the three. You dig your

Plate 11: The south-facing terrace showing the wonderful view to the Downs

Plate 12: Steps up and brick paving to the west end of the terrace

hole, remembering as you do so its relationship in size to its surroundings. Do make enough room so that you can walk all round it easily and elegantly. Try and visualise, as you position it, where the fountain is to be and what the jet of the fountain will show up against—dark foliage is best, but so site the fountain that sunshine will enliven the jet of water. I have so contrived one vista in my garden that you can see the jet of the fountain from a dark avenue of trees—so that the fountain is at the end of the tunnel in the sun. A fair way behind it—20 ft. or so—is a group of pampas grass (*Cortaderia sellona*) with its long leaves falling as water and shining in the sun. (It spoils the effect I think when the Pampas flowers!)

Decide how deep the pond is to be—this can be decided on the size of your dogs if they fall in, or the size and age of your children or grandchildren (terrifying tragedies can occur in seconds of inattention, for the flashing of the gaudy fish will magnetise the youngest of toddlers). The depth, if you are childless or dogless, can be decided by the kind of water lilies you will want to grow. The shallowest for the smallest water lily (*Nymphaea*) is about 6 in., and the deepest you will require—and you'll need a great area, too—is 3 ft.

As a general rule the largest *nymphaea* are only suitable for the larger pools and the small ones for small pools, or the shallow edges and corners of large pools. If a small pool has been made very deep you can plant your small lily in a basket which you elevate on bricks. It is sometimes stated that water lilies will grow in water 4–6 ft. deep—maybe they will after a great deal of time, but not initially. Allow when digging, not only for the depth of the concrete (if it is to be a concrete pool) but also for the depth of soil at the bottom of your pond and a layer of pebbles or sand above it. For the proper well-being of fish in the winter there should be a depth of at least 18 in. They need this depth for their seasonal rest.

I do not like iris or similar spear-shaped plants at the edges of a formal pool. I only like to have the plates of a water lily and other totally submerged foliage. This is purely a personal fad and quite possibly because I am lucky enough to have a natural pool as well (and a lake under construction). But my view is that the reed-like plants by the side of the formal pool, which has a hard stone edge, not only spoils the shape of the pool but the reeds look like country bumpkins in smocks (should there be such folk today!) in the midst of Trafalgar Square.

Your formal pool these days can be of concrete, plastic

sheeting or fibre glass. PVC or Butyl rubber sheeting pools are best suited if the pool is round or oval with easy curves and no sharp edges or corners. Butyl rubber rectangular pools can be ordered prefabricated for single depth pools. Both these materials require no further treatment after the pool is filled with water before the introduction of plants and fish. The same is true with fibre glass pools.

Select a level piece of ground, sited if possible in full sunshine, and away from trees—but if your pond is large the reflection of a tree like a weeping willow is half its enjoyment! Excavate the pool, firming the soil with a rammer and removing (if it is not to be a concrete pool) all stones and sharp objects. If you are using a liner, cover the bottom with sand or sifted soil. Place the liner evenly over the excavation, stretched fairly tightly with stones, bricks, paving or members of the family distributed at frequent intervals so that when you add the water the liner will immerse evenly. Start to fill slowly with water. The weight of the water will take the liner to the bottom of the pool and you will have allowed a large border of sheeting to stay level round the top edge. You need to leave a flap of about a foot or so all round which will then be held permanently by the paving slabs placed formally or informally round the edge according to the kind of pool you are making. The best effect is achieved if the stones overlap the edge of the pool by about a couple of inches.

If the pool is to be of fibre glass make your hole the size and shape of the fibre glass pool you have bought, put in the pool, make sure it fits snugly and then put your slabs round the edge.

If the pool is to be concreted, when you have finished digging ram the bottom of the pond firmly and then pour on a layer of 3 in. of concrete, made of one part cement to three parts sand. When this is dry and hard—after perhaps a day—but if it is a very fine, hot, sunny day cover the concrete with damp sacks so that it will not crack—you can make the sides, for which you will need wood screening which you will put on the bottom, 4 in. from the earth side, and fill with cement, ramming it well in so that there are no air pockets. Leave for two days. Then place your paving round the top of the pool and fill with water. If you get cracks in a concrete pool these can be sealed with a plastic bituminous compound harmless to plants and fish, which can also be used if you have any need to seal the side corners or where your sides meet the bottom. This compound is supplied by most aquatic suppliers.

For concrete pools a small outlet pipe should be made from

the top of the pool under the paving edge to drain surplus rain or flood water to a soakaway. Gas piping is usually adequate, though a land drain is often better as frogs sometimes clog, get stuck and die in small pipes. Concrete pools should be filled with water and kept filled for about six months and emptied before you plant any plants in the pool, to soak out the acids and poisons in the cement. The plants should then all be well-established and growing so that they are giving off oxygen into the water before the fish are introduced.

At the bottom of the pool you will place 6 in. of good loam and if this is then covered with washed sand and gravel—preferably taken from a quickly-running stream—then you stand a better chance of clear water. Put in about 6 in. of water, but do it slowly and into a receptacle placed on the bottom of the pond so that you do not disturb the soil. If you are tempted to use manure for the water lilies, this must be very old cow manure and turned several times over six months with the loam. The lily is then set with its crown or growing point just clear of the soil. Planting of all water plants is best done in May or June. It is advisable not to fill the pond completely after planting but to put in a little more each week, so long as you cover the crowns with water immediately. If the pond is already full, lower the lily in a container on a brick plinth which should be shortened week by week as growth develops. Some lilies will not flower the first year; they are white, yellow, pink and red. It is nice to have all four colours if you can. *Nymphaea virginalis* is the largest white flowering variety, with large double white flowers—excellent for a large pool (depth $1\frac{1}{2}$—$2\frac{1}{2}$ ft.). For a medium-sized pool *N. marliacea* 'Albida' is excellent, for small pools 'Odorata Alba' and 'Candida'; for a tiny pool or tub *N. pygmaea* 'Alba'.

N. col 'A. J. Welch' is canary-yellow for medium pools. For smaller pools, *N. odorata* 'Sulphurea', with mottled leaves and sulphur-yellow flowers is excellent, and more orange than yellow is *N. solfatare*. *N. pygmaea* 'Helvola', with tiny flowers, is for a tiny pool—with no tiny fishing gnomes, please!

N. masaniello is a rich carmine-rose; suitable for deeper, larger pools. *N. marliacea* 'Carnea' for medium pools, and *N. odorata* 'Turicensis' is the pink one for smaller pools. The red water-lily for a large pool is *N.* 'Chas de Meurville' with wine-red blooms. For medium pools, the finest red is *N.* 'Escarboncle'. For small pools *N.* 'Rene Gerard' has rich rose-crimson flowers.

There must now be some submerged plants in the pool for

oxygenation and purification of the water. *Ranunculus aquatilis* (Water Crowsfoot) has fern-like underwater foliage and on the surface a mass of snow-white buttercup-like flowers. *Vallsineria spiralis* has long tape-like leaves and is often seen in aquaria. *Myriophyllum spicatum* is the Spiked Milfoil and has finely divided foliage in colour green, via bronze to a bronzy-red. *Ceratophyllum demersum* (Hornwort) has dark green tufted foliage a little like thick green tassels and is good for oxygenating the water.

For the informal pool or lakeside, there are the following suitable plants. *Caltha palustris* is the Marsh Marigold or King Cup. *C. p.* 'Plena' is the Double Marsh Marigold. *Hypericum elodes* has downy foliage and yellow musk-like flowers; it is the Marsh St John's Wort. *Mentha aquatica* is the Water Mint with mauve flowers and a pungent minty odour when trodden on. *Myosotis palustris* is the Water Forget-me-not with the familiar blue flowers, fewer and darker than the garden myosotis. *Alisma plantago* is the Great Water Plantain. *Iris kaempferi* 'Variegata' has rich purple blooms and variegated foliage. *Iris pseudacorus* is the Yellow Flag Iris growing wild in Sussex ponds. *Iris sibirica* has vivid blue flowers on erect stems. *Lysimachia vulgaris* is Orange Loosestrife. The American Skunk Cabbage (*Lysichitum americanum*) has flowers like a yellow wild arum lily and the quaintest thinnest black roots like human hair; I hated planting mine. *Typha latifolia* is the bullrush, and is very much for the large pool only; it grows 6–7 ft. high and multiplies like mad.

The most usual fish to keep are goldfish. These come in various varieties—the Fantail goldfish is beautiful with large fancy tails hanging gracefully in grotesque shapes, and often has large, protruding eyes. The Shubunkin is a smooth goldfish with no scales. All the goldfish come in colours ranging from black, black and gold, black and silver, bronze, red, orange and silver. They range in size from about an inch to very nearly a foot. They breed easily and so many emerge from so many eggs that in spite of the fry being eaten by the larger fish, many will survive and populate the pool. An inch of fish is supposed to be allowed for a square foot of surface of the pond, but with plenty of lilies and oxygenating plants and a fountain to help with the oxygenation this rule can be well exceeded. Golden and silver orfe are quick, elegant fish which move more quickly than goldfish and are more like rudd in shape. They come in similar sizes to goldfish and will often swim round in shoals. A couple of tench, dark green fish which keep well to the bottom of the pond, are very useful as scavenging fish to help with the pond's 'balance'. Water snails (*Mollusca*) also help with keeping a pond clear, feeding, as they do, on the algae and decaying plant life. It is best to introduce them after the plants are well established as they are inclined to feed on young new shoots.

Fish are inactive, very nearly moribund, in the winter and get more active and more hungry as the water warms to mid-summer. It is then that they need feeding with natural food like water fleas (*Daphnia*) and all the other minute aquatic insects, larvae, and tiny life almost like bacteria, called infusoria. Daphnia and infusoria can be obtained in cans from aquatic suppliers. So can dried fish food. You must be very careful only to give as much of this as the fish will eat at one time, as it is decaying matter of this kind which will pollute a pond and cause disease and discomfort to the fish.

A pool which is balanced with its plant life and its fishes and snails and food will have clear water. It is when a pond is first started that it gets very green and one despairs of ever cleaning the thick algae. Heavy algae growth should be removed with a rake. If you are greatly troubled with green opaque water for too long it is best to get a special preparation formulated to control and prevent its growth. It is perfectly safe to use and will not harm fish or plants.

If your pond is large and deep, then icing presents no problem. With a small fish pool thin ice occasionally can also be ignored. Long periods of thick ice on a small pool can kill the fish; not with the actual cold but because, even in their semi-dormant state, they must have oxygen. The rotting of the winter vegetation in a pond produces gases which must escape. The oxygenating plants are also dormant so that if the thick ice is left sealing the gases in, and keeping out the oxygen from outside, then the fish deteriorate and eventually will die. The vibration caused by the breaking of thick ice is bad for fish, and for the sides of the pool! A hole at the side made by hot water from a kettle is a good way. There are small electric immersion heaters sold for ponds. A rubber ball kept floating on the water helps to stop the formation of ice. So does a log of wood.

The best fountains are motored with fountain pumps which feature an electric motor sealed into a plastic block to keep the water from it and to electrically insulate it. These can be bought for both fountains and waterfalls. I strongly advise the fitting of the items by an experienced electrician as water and electricity can be very dangerous companions especially when children and pets are about. This is a job for a fully qualified expert.

Fountains do complete a pool and are so cool sounding on a very hot day. Don't plant your lilies immediately under a fountain as the constant dripping may inhibit the growth—that is if you are going to have the fountain playing for long periods.

Fountains are not turned on, you notice. They play. It is such an apt term.

With a water-mill it is important to keep the water flowing past either through the weir or over the wheel, or both. Water will always surprise you. In June 2 in. of rain can fall in a couple of hours and flood you. Constant watch has to be kept. Also, it is necessary to keep all streams and inlets clear of weeds and kept at their proper width, and not allowed to silt up. The banks of the mill pond must be kept trim and not allowed to cave in; cattle must not be allowed to stamp the banks down and the pond must be dredged, at intervals so that it is deep enough to contain flood water. All of these items I found out on taking over a neglected mill. There were times when I came home, perhaps from performing a late cabaret at the Savoy, at two in the morning, and found it necessary to put gumboots on and climb out over the wheel (twelve feet from the ground) and ease out a 'leaf' (a piece of wood the size and shape and weight of a railway sleeper) with a spade, letting the water swirl around me at terrific speed in the eerie light of a hurricane lamp! To avoid this sort of crisis all your water must be moving and/or contained in immaculate banks. A good way to preserve a bank, I found, was to insert a foot deep into the ground and under water, a length of chestnut paling which was then cut off level with the top of the bank.

The reflection of the sun and the clouds in the water; the tiny voles, the herons, the itinerant swans, the swoopings and divings of the swallows—the mystery of the autumnal mist on the water—all these give an added beauty and delight with the addition of another element to your garden—water.

15 Walls and Climbers

If your garden is small, not an inch of wall space must be wasted. The house must not be covered, as brickwork is attractive, but a whole lot of the house can be made to flower at different times of the year, providing interest and fragrance. Similarly, if your garden is small, there will be fences and hedges to cover and make the most of. The screen block walling made of perforated cement blocks is very popular today and if used as a media for clothing with climbing plants, will marry into any garden scheme attractively.

CLEMATIS is the most popular climber of them all. It is an easy plant to grow. Those which flower on the current year's growth need to be pruned hard every spring and the others which flower on the previous year's growth need light pruning after flowering. There is a mysterious disease called clematis 'wilt' which affects the larger flowered garden hybrids (*jackmanii*). You can glory in the sight of a flower-laden clematis half-way up your house in the morning and in the evening it will have collapsed and died. They do like lime and it helps all clematis to have a cool root run; either cover the roots with a large slab of stone or shade with low-growing shrubs. You also buy them as pot grown plants and can put them in (with care and attention to watering) at almost any time of the year. Interest these days does centre round the more showy hybrid clematis but the species, as in roses, are well worth attention. *C. flammula* is a pleasantly scented autumn-flowering clematis; it has a small white flower. *C. cirrhosa*, not too hardy, is evergreen and produces its greenish bell-shaped flowers in winter, commencing at the end of January. It must have a sheltered position from winds, preferably on a wall. *C. montana* is a rampant grower, with white flowers in spring. There is a rich pink form, *C. m.* 'Elizabeth' which is fragrant, and *C. m.* 'Rubens', a deep pink form. *C. macropetela* has double starry-blue flowers flushed with purple in the spring. *C. m.* 'Alba' is white and *C. m.* 'Markhamii' is lavender-pink. It is not very tall—about 8 ft.

and flowers in the spring. *C. tangutica* and *C. orientalis* are yellow, the first with glaucous foliage and bell-shaped flowers, and the second is scented.

Of the large-flowered hybrids, 'Ville de Lyon' is bright carmine and very floriferous; *C.* 'Vyvian Pennell' is deep violet-blue and has double flowers from May to July. 'The President' is deep violet; 'Nellie Moser' is light mauve with a red bar down the petals and flowers most generously from May to September. *C.* 'Gipsy Queen' is a rich violet-purple; she flowers from July to October. *C. jackmanii* is violet-blue from July to September. There are many, many other named varieties —see them at the Chelsea Show and take your pick. As they are always sold in pots, take your pick when they are flowering!

Chimonanthus fragrans—the Winter Sweet—grows to 6–8 ft. with sweetly-scented flowers in mid-winter—it does best on a sunny wall. I once had it growing behind a wood-shed and under a kitchen window in quite a shady place—here the delightful scent vied with less appetising smells from indoors—but it made a joy of the chore of getting logs on a cold January day.

Forsythia suspensa is the graceful climbing kind—it does not have so many bright open yellow flowers (these look down, rather like a snowdrop) as *F. spectabilis* or *F. s.* 'Beatrix Farrand', with extra large flowers. A little bit similar, in that the flowers are yellow and star-like, is *Jasminum nudiflorum*, the Winter Jasmine, whose fragrant blossoms are with us from December to May. *J. stephanense* is a fragrant pink and is not much grown.

For a north wall, with moist acid soil, and quite hardy, from Chile, comes *Lapageria rosea* with waxen crimson trumpets.

LONICERA are the honeysuckles, of which I have already written. *L. halliana*, the evergreen is creamy-yellow, most odiferous, flowers, from July to October. Do not forget *L. japonica* 'Aureoreticulata', with light green leaves netted and veined with yellow, but no flowers. *L. caprifolium* has leaves like those of a baby eucalyptus.

The Passion Flower—*Passiflora caerulea*, has fragrant blue flowers—is rather tender but grows so luxuriantly with me in Sussex on a south wall that it never flowers. The solution to the mystery is, I'm told, for me to confine the roots in a large pot so that it gets potbound and will then flower. If you live in the north you must grow this in a cool greenhouse. It is edible if you are very hungry—not for the fleshy outside but for the seed and the jelly-like substance around it. There is a shadowy white variety for the white garden, *P. c.* 'Constance Elliott'.

The Russian Vine, *Polygonum baldschuanicum*, comes from

Bokhara with the carpets, for it is not Russian at all; it is vigorous and quite cheap, too.

All the climbing roses are lovely and I have described some of them to you. The yellow climbing rose which used to be called 'Hidcote' is now known as 'Laurence Johnstone' after the designer of the garden, and is certainly one of the best yellow roses for climbing that I know.

SCHIZOPHRAGMA is the climbing hydrangea and not to be confused with *Hydrangea petiolaris*.

I'm not very keen on the climbing potato, *Solanum crispum*, with lavender or white flowers in autumn, because it looks like a lank summer jasmine without the scent!

There are various vines for climbing—fruiting ones and ones with very attractive foliage (what vine has not got attractive foliage, and what a lovely way to present your guests with fruit like strawberries, raspberries, peaches than on the platter of an enormous vine leaf. You will have to use a plate under it!). *Vitis coignetiae* is a robustious creeper with large rounded leaves with good autumn colouring, but you will have to support it. It is not the virginia creeper, which is self-clinging and will roam all over your house—this is called *Parthenocissus quinquefolia*—or to be old-fashioned *Vitis quinquefolia*. Then there is the more 'maple leaved' one, *P. tricuspidata*, also self-clinging with glossy leaves that colour well in the autumn.

If you grow a vine, why not grow one for the grapes? Or, better still, to make your own wine from. You need a light soil—Gloucestershire, Worcestershire, Kent and Surrey were the great wine-growing counties in the times of the monasteries. Your vine needs to face south or west. Once you have achieved the growing of your vine up its support, side shoots will grow which will produce buds which will again develop into side shoots. It is from these that the fruit will appear, and if you want good-sized fruit you must limit these so that they appear about a foot apart. When one of these laterals is about 6 in. long a flower shoot will grow with a growing 'tip'. If you let this flower mature into fruit you must then nip the tip off (sounds like a racing hint) leaving a couple of leaves above the cluster of flowers. Once the vine is in regular fruit you must feed it liberally with liquid manure. Then with scissors you thin the fruit, but not, I think, if you are just letting the fruit grow for ornament or fun. If you are growing for alcoholic fun, then you will need to thin out, ensuring that the centre of the cluster is free from tiny fruit, but leaving the rest round the edges, as it were, to mature.

The famous vine at Hampton Court is a Black Hamburgh so there is no reason why you should not grow one of these outside. For a white grape, grow Royal Muscadine or Muscatel. *Vinifera purpurea* is the claret vine, and will give you bunches of dark blue fruit—and the leaves turn purple in the late summer and red in the autumn. It needs a south wall to be kind enough to do all this for you.

If you want to grow a vine for decoration, let it grow willy-nilly and train it over whatever wall, pillar, fence or what-have-you to be covered! If you are keen on the grapes as well, you must prune it hard back to a single bud, or perhaps two buds for the first three years to give the vine a good strong stock. This is done in the autumn. Then when you have a strong 'trunk' about 2 in. round the stem, you can let it go and it will cover the side of your house. Don't climb up the ladder to thin out your fifth year's crop after you have partaken of your fourth year's vintage. You may fall off!

HEDERA—the ivies. All are self-clinging and hardy and some of the variegated ones are very showy. Use them as ground cover or climbers. *H. canariensis* 'Variegata' needs a sheltered wall. *Hedera colchica* 'Dentato Variegata' grows rapidly. The ivies love a poor soil.

A house covered with WISTERIA is a magnificent sight. If you want to sell your house then you will do so easily when the wisteria is in flower. It grows much more quickly than you imagine it will do. There are two kinds; I wonder if Lewis Carroll knew this—if he did it would have delighted him! One kind, *W. floribunda*, has stems which twine clockwise and *W. sinensis* has stems which twine anti-clockwise. It is not fussy about soil but it does like moisture. The flowers are produced in long racemes like laburnum; they are mauve and fragrant. There is also a clockwise and anti-clockwise white—'Alba'. There is also *W. floribunda* 'Oosthock's Blue', which is blue, but I must say I prefer mine mauve—or as the catalogues say, light lilac-blue.

CEANOTHUS is good for walls. So are the Pyracanthas. *Tropaeolum speciosum* planted on the shady side of a hedge (yew) in acid soil is spectacular if you can get it to grow. Scotsmen always can—in Scotland that is!

The Morello Cherry is excellent for a north wall, both for blossom and the shiny fruit which is good for cooking and jams. The apricot, peach and nectarine can also be grown against walls facing south in certain areas. Figs, too, are successful in the southern counties, given the shelter of a wall.

16 Annuals and Biennials

If you are creating a new garden then expense is of prime importance, and so is the desire for immediate results. Sometimes your requirement is for a temporary effect—a mass of flowers in a part of the garden which in time will become, as your plan evolves, something else, and in the meantime you dislike seeing it as a bare space. Your remedy in these predicaments is to sow annuals, and half-hardy annuals. Annuals are grown by sowing out-of-doors from March till June in the place where the plants are to flower. Some can be sown in the autumn to flower in the following early summer, but all annual plants die after flowering. Half-hardy annuals include most of the summer bedding groups; they are usually sown under glass, raised under glass, and then planted out in the open garden when there is no longer a danger of frost. Some can be sown out-of-doors later in the season but they will have a short growing life as the first autumn frost will cut them down. Biennials are sown one year to flower the next and are then discarded, although some, such as Sweet Williams and the biennial verbascums, can be used for several seasons.

The general cultural procedure if you have the time is to dig the ground over well in the autumn so that the frost can get at the soil and break it down, and then to sow in the spring where plants are to bloom. No manure is required so long as the soil is in good heart, as annuals often prefer to flourish on a poor soil. Compost always helps a poor soil in texture and substance, and remember you will need a fine tilth for sowing. After hoeing and raking the soil to provide this fine tilth, you can sow the seed broadcast over the area where you need your plants to grow, or in drills—that is to say, very small trenches over the same area. It is essential to sow the seeds thinly and never deeply—the ground should only just cover them. Indeed with some of the very fine seeds there is no need to cover at all. When the seedlings are an inch or so high thin them out a few inches apart, choosing to leave the strongest and more vigorous seedlings. Then subsequent thinning out should eventually leave your remaining plants spaced out at about threequarters of their final height (e.g. a plant that is going to finish up to 1 ft. in height should be 9 in. apart from its fellows). It always seems to me a great pity to throw the seedlings away, so long as you do your thinning out in showery weather when the seedlings are small, you can transplant these thinnings to some other part of the garden. If your garden is on a windy site you must place twigs at intervals amongst the plants. These supports will be hidden when the plants are fully grown. Hazel twigs (short lengths of pea sticks) and brushwood are the ideal material.

All the following are easy annuals to grow and can be bought in packets costing approximately 5p or 6p each. The height is always mentioned on the packet, together with any special cultural instructions—and of course there is always the most seductive and highly coloured picture of the contents in full exotic bloom.

ALYSSUM is usually white as well as lilac-pink and violet —these newer coloured varieties being much smaller than the white and if sown thickly make a good mat of colour for a bare patch in a new rockery. *Anchusa capensis* is like a large Forget-Me-Not. BARTONIA with flowers like a St Johns Wort. CALENDULA, the pot marigold, is an old-fashioned flower with many new hybrids and refinements. COREOPSIS in the annual form. CAMPANULA, deep violet-blue and useful for edging. CANDYTUFT, whose seeds can be bought in self colours or a mixture, and with several sowings a season will provide constant colour—they grow in great profusion anywhere. The annual CHRYSANTHEMUM is similarly vigorous, but it does need support. It has brightly banded tri-colour flowers. *Clarkia elegans* has tall graceful sprays of double flowers and they too need support. *Convolvulus major* is the Morning Glory, a blue flowered climber to cover trellis. CORNFLOWER is the annual, ranging from 3 ft. in height down to the dwarf varieties—the colours ranging from white, pink through mauve to blue. COSMOS is a tall fern-like annual with white and pink flowers and there is now a yellow five-petalled variety.

DIMORPHOTHECA is a South African annual which grows quickly from seed and needs a sunny position—it is a daisy-like flower and the Aurantiaca hybrids range in colour from white through the yellows to orange and salmon-orange. ESCH-

SCHOLTZIA is the Californian Poppy. It used to be orange or yellow but now there are the Harlequin hybrids from Carters with a grand variety of shades ranging from yellow and orange through pink and red to almost mauve with buffs and beiges. There is a new kind brought out by Messrs. Dobies called 'Ballerina' which is double and fluted, and has in most cases variegated flowers.

GODETIAS have been vastly improved too in the last few years—the dwarf bedding godetia being useful for edgings and to fill in empty spots in the rock garden. The godetia needs sun. There are the azalea-flowered kinds, including a blue one, and there are tall varieties which are useful for cutting. If I owned a hotel and needed flowers in a small pot for each table in the dining room, I would grow a succession of godetias the whole summer through. GYPSOPHILA is a plant I would grow for the same purpose. It is a complementary flower—like a feathery fern might be—to other flowers in an arrangement, and in the border it makes a most interesting mound of dainty pure white or pink flowers. You sow it the previous September to give you early flowers, and then from March to June to give a succession throughout the season.

LARKSPURS are the annual delphinium and there are some magnificent new strains of great size with long stems for cutting. Here again, sow in September. There are also dwarf varieties for edgings or a windy site.

LAVATERA grows from 3½–4 ft. in height, and has quite large hibiscus-like flowers of cerise-pink. It is an admirable plant for the odd bare patch at the back of an herbaceous border, and good to grow amongst lupins which will be over in July. The lavatera then comes in profusion of flower in August.

Once you have LIMNANTHES you will have it for ever; for it flowers most generously with yellow flowers edged with white, 9 in. high, and fern-like foliage. It will flower in one glorious blaze and quickly go to seed. You then pull it out and replace with some late summer bedding plant—in the meantime, unknown to you, it will have seeded itself everywhere and you will have a carpet of young seedlings. This is the way I use it. It is sown late in the summer so that it is up and forms a ground cover for spring bulbs like hyacinths or tulips. When they are over, the limnanthes blooms. Out it comes and fuchsias are put into the bed. Then, as the fuchsias bloom for the rest of the summer, the new seedlings are allowed to grow, and when the fuchsias are brought in in the autumn, the limnanthes is up and ready, self-sown, to be the ground cover for the next lot of spring bulbs. I do this in one square bed I have in a little court-yard.

LINARIA is toadflax. The wild one is yellow, a sort of in-ferior snapdragon, but the cultivated hybrids include, in colour: yellow, orange, crimson, pink, blue and violet, all about a foot high. There is a dwarf kind called 'Fairy Bouquet'.

LINUM is the Scarlet Flax. The seeds are linseed-like and the flower a little like a single pink. It is very free flowering and will grow anywhere and quickly. It is a good seed for a child to sow because, like candytuft and virginia stock, it gives a quick colourful result. There is no hanging about.

LOVE-LIES-BLEEDING (*Amaranthus candatus*) is a plant much used by flower arrangers. It is very good for the tops of walls so that its long dangling tassels can drape themselves over the edge. They have an odd Victorian look about them. The crimson one has slightly reddish leaves too, particularly when young; the green one has light green tassels: sometimes these drooping furry tassels are longer than the plant is high, if I make myself crystal clear? And this is why I plant them near the edge of a wall so that they may hang over.

MALOPE has mallow-like flowers of red, rose, white or crimson and is about 3 ft. high with trumpet-shaped flowers.

MIGNONETTE has odd greenish flowers with a reddish tinge to them, and you would never have it in your garden except for its glorious fragrance. It has spinach-like leaves and, now I come to think of it, if you allow spinach to go to seed the fragrance is glorious, so perhaps they are related. You may smell your spinach but don't eat your *Reseda odorata* because this relationship is only supposition and it may be poisonous. It is certainly a bit choosy for whom and where it grows. 'Machet' has large yellow and red heads, 'Orange Queen' is orange, 'Crimson Fragrance' has broad spikes of reddish flowers. It is 12 in. high.

The NASTURTIUM comes from South America. It has been transformed in recent years. It used only to be a quick climber with flowers of yellow and vermilion. Now it can be dwarf, or double or fragrant to order and its range in colour is from yellow via orange and mahogany to the deepest crimson—with sometimes a shaded or spotted effect. But no matter what kind you choose it grows quickly in a sunny position and the poorer the soil the more blooms you will get. There is also the Canary Creeper which is *Tropaeolum peregrinum* and has pale green leaves and crenellated canary-yellow flowers, on a vigorous climber which is excellent to cover trellis in a single summer.

NIGELLA is the famous annual also called Love-in-a-Mist. The 'Love' being the blue flower 'in-a-Mist' of fern-like foliage. Alas, you can now get rose pink, white and a dirty dark mauve as well, but I am more than happy to stick to blue.

The annual and biennial POPPIES should all be sown where they are to grow and then thinned out as they do not transplant happily. There are many different kinds: carnation-flowered, paeony-flowered and the Shirley poppies. All of these have a wide range and are about 2 ft. high. The Iceland Poppy has open cup-shaped flowers ranging from white to yellow, orange, salmon and rose. It is difficult to decide the best way to treat the sowing of Iceland poppies. Some people do so in April and then thin out; others sow in June in a nursery bed with the wallflowers and Sweet Williams and Canterbury Bells, and then move to their flowering positions in October, which is the only time they will put up with disturbance. Please move them on a damp day.

My wife adores SAPONARIA so I grow it. If she did not, I would not. It is pink and good for cutting. It has graceful sprays which do not quite go with its old English name of Cowherb.

There are annual SALVIAS, one of which is called Thistle Sage and has felted grey hairs on its leaves. *S. horminum* comes from the Mediterranean and has coloured bracts of deep violet blue, or pink, or white; all good for cutting.

SWEET SULTAN is a kind of annual cornflower with fringed flowers of every colour except blue.

The annual SUNFLOWER is a magnificent giant redolent of old cottage gardens, and very useful if you have an aviary as the seed heads are enormous. The various varieties range from 4 ft. to 7–8 ft. in height. I grow them against a wall with hollyhocks. When they are in need of water they look down on you in a scornful way, and when you have watered them they raise their heads to the sun and grow and grow and grow. No wonder Van Gogh could not stop painting them.

Half-hardy annuals are best sown in pots or boxes in a warm greenhouse or frame during February and March. The seedlings are then pricked out into other pots or boxes and are still kept in the warmth till April. In April and May they are gradually hardened off, but you cannot put them out into the open garden until all danger of frost is passed. One sees so many half-hardy annuals offered in boxes by shops in April whilst there is still a possibility of frost and you should, to my mind, not buy them until you can plant them out. Any interruption in their growth will spoil them and their chances of being 100% successful as flowering plants. This goes for letting them get too dry as well.

Let us go quickly through a list of the most popular of the half-hardy annuals.

AGERATUM has fluffy lavender blue heads grown in great profusion. 'Blue Bouquet' is $1\frac{1}{2}$ ft. high and good for cutting. If you remove the dead heads ageratum will flower continuously from June to October. There are several hybrid varieties from 8 in. in height. They make a splendid edging plant.

ANTIRRHINUMS are perennial but best treated as half-hardy annuals. They grow slowly and you must get your seed into boxes in February. There are many new varieties but the older, taller, fuller kinds are coming back into fashion. They are often subject to a rust disease and you should make sure if your area is subject to rust and then to buy only a rust resistant strain.

The CHINA ASTER is invaluable to keep your flower show going well into late summer. It needs to be sown in March. Here again, as with the antirrhinums, there are many hybrid varieties ranging from dwarf ones to Hercules, doubles, singles ostrich-plumed, and every colour of white, pink and blue—and in the Aster 'Unicorn' variety there is a yellow.

ARCTOTIS is a native of South Africa and therefore needs a dry sunny position. They are brilliant in colour, quick in flowering and good for cutting with exotic colourings of red, orange, yellow, apricot, carmine, cream and white.

The fibrous rooted BEGONIA should be treated as a half-hardy annual and are some of the most effective and floriferous plants for edging and bedding.

The *Cleome pungens* has large pink spider-like flowers and grows to 3 ft. high. It looks so like a well-established perennial that you can hardly imagine that it can be such a splendid plant in a half summer's growth. 'Rose Queen' is the variety.

COSMOS (see also Hardy Annuals) has beautiful feathery foliage and grows to 3 ft. There are also what are known as Dwarf Klondyke types. White and rose pink are the traditional colours but there are some new hybrids with yellows and oranges called 'Bright Lights'.

DELPHINIUMS can be treated as a half-hardy annual. You can then get your flowers later in the summer when blues are at a premium—these are the *Chinensis* varieties and not to be confused with the rocket larkspur.

Plate 13 (*top*): The 'Orangery'. My office leads in to this—which has heating attached to the house central heating; we can grow most house plants in winter and summer

Plate 14 (*bottom*): Close-up of the pond on the terrace

Plate 15 (*top*): This lawn overlooks the courtyard shown in Plate 9. The different levels again give interest. In the distance is the quick-grown shrubbery

Plate 16 (*bottom*): This is a well-head designed and constructed by Mr Francis Essex for his garden in Bedfordshire to cover the main drainage manhole in his garden. Notice the ironwork done by a local blacksmith and also the excellent way in which the whole structure fits the scene and is suitably large and important

COLTNESS DAHLIAS are treated as a half-hardy annual, and by the end of the summer you will have tubers for use the following season.

ANNUAL PINKS—especially *Dianthus* 'Persian Carpet' make a very good fill-in for bare patches in the rock garden. They are excellent for patches in paving and for edging.

HELICHRYSUM are everlasting flowers which when cut and dried (hang upside down) will make excellent flower arrangements for the winter.

HELIOTROPE is the Cherry Pie, with deliciously scented flowers. Their scent goes well, as does their colour, with eucalyptus. I plant some round the feet of my trees and on a hot summer day the aroma is overpowering. *H. arborescens* 'Giganteum' grows to 2 ft. high. There is a new short hollyhock (treat as a half-hardy annual) with silvery-pink flowers, which would look well with the giant heliotrope.

LOBELIA goes with alyssum. Or it used to. It still does, I am afraid, for the unimaginative. Its chief value is in the fact that it flowers continuously for the whole season. It is useful for the front of a border in drifts or patches. The trailing varieties are useful in dry walls or for hanging baskets. Alyssum, which I have already mentioned, is often used alternatively as edging or for bedding with lobelia. A Victorian fashion which dies hard. Used as a very wide edging of 2–3 ft. wide it makes a spectacular drift.

The double AFRICAN MARIGOLD, the FRENCH MARIGOLD and the tinier, daintier TAGETES are all much the same family, and all have had considerable attention from the seedsmen. You can get many shades of colour in the orange, mahogany, yellow range and they range in height from 2 ft. to 9 in. You sow the seed in heat in March and prick out, when big enough, into other boxes. You then plant out when the frosts are over into their permanent positions, when they will flower from July onwards.

MESEMBRYANTHEMUM are only for dry and sunny positions; they only open their flowers to the sun. The leaves are cactus-like and the plant comes from South Africa. The flowers are daisy-like and about 2 in. across, ranging in colour from white through pink, red, yellow, orange and purple. Do be very careful as you transplant them from the box into the garden; the plant is quite sturdy and heavy but the stem which joins the leaves to the root is threadlike and needs great care when planting to ensure that you do not break it.

NEMESIA is a quick-growing small plant of 9 in. or so in

many colours used for edging. It has a long flowering season and is popular.

NICOTIANA is the tobacco plant. It is much improved these days, in that it will flower during the day as well as at dusk; but it is in the evenings that one notices the heavy fragrance. There is a lime-green flowering variety now that is in great demand by flower arrangers. If you are on a windy site tobacco plants are prone to falling over, so use the new dwarf varieties.

PENTSTEMONS are magnificent plants, and sown in a heated frame or greenhouse from January to March will give a wonderful display from July to late summer; then bring them in to the shelter of your frame for the winter.

PETUNIAS can now be bought in all shapes and sizes and colours. There are many F1 hybrids, and one can also now get pelleted seeds to ensure that none are wasted. The giant all-double petunias are most attractive. I use a pink one which has a salmon tinge to it with *Cineraria maritima* to bed-out a small corner. If you have a wet summer, petunias can look sadder than a drenched holidaymaker at the seaside; in a fine summer there is no more magnificent flower. How do you decide? Do you get your crystal-ball out, one wonders?

The annual PHLOX—*Phlox drummondii* has brightly coloured clusters of flowers and is an excellent bedding out plant. It is easy and continuously flowering. There are dwarf kinds of 6–8 in. and large-flowered varieties up to 51 in. These need a few twigs between them here and there to make sure they stand up.

The GLORIOSA DAISIES are a late summer delight and the giant tetraploid hybrids are especial favourites of mine, with large single flowers 6 in. across, with conical centres and stiff stems. The colours are yellow and dark brown and chestnut and mahogany red, and the petals are the texture of fine velvet. If these flowers had fragrance then how magnificent they would be. The hybridists and nurserymen are clever today with the many forms of dwarf, tall, double, etc., etc., in endless variation; they are clever too with their colour combinations, I wonder if it ever occurs to them to develop perfume in flowers which do not have it. What a challenge to create a richly scented dahlia.

'Bonfire' SALVIA, as we call it in our family, is a good stand-by for creating a patch of brilliant red in the summer garden which will go on from June to October. 'Blaze of Fire' is the current name. *Salvia patens* is intense gentian blue. SCABIOUS can be either treated as a half-hardy annual or a biennial.

SALPIGLOSSIS is a much improved flower, as we have seen at recent Chelsea Shows. They are now 2 ft. high with richly veined flowers, all colours from blue, yellow brown and pink, and looking as exotic as an orchid. STATICE is a half-hardy annual from the sea-shore. There are many pastel shades and they are not only attractive in the garden but as a dried flower they are a flower arranger's delight.

NIGHT-SCENTED STOCKS as we used to call them, some coming in miserable single bloomed spires and some very beautiful double flowered spires, all have a much prized perfume, particularly on a still damp day in mid-summer. Now you sow in gentle heat and the seedlings are a light or a dark green; the dark ones are singles, so you ruthlessly remove these and the light green-leaved seedlings grow up to be the desired exotic double-flowered blooms. You get them in packets of mixed colours and you get packets of a definite shade, so that in bedding schemes you can be very selective and artistic. The lavender ones go well with a blue border, and the white ones are very valuable to fill in bare patches of a white garden. Seed can also be sown in a frame in June for winter sweet flowers in the greenhouse.

VERBENA grows in attractive clusters a little like Sweet William but with smaller florets. There is every colour of the rainbow, and I am very fond of these modest little flowers which, if sown under glass in the spring and planted out after the frosts have gone, make excellent edging or filling-in patches for the front of the border. The plants suffer very much if their growth is checked in any way, so please be generous and plant fairly closely together. There are dwarf varieties growing only 6 in. high.

ZINNIAS need a dry summer and they are not too pleased with being transplanted from their boxes in the greenhouse to their beds in the garden. The smallest of the jiffy-pots is my answer to this dilemma, and then the plants need not go out until June when all risk of cold wet May nights is over. There is nothing so miserable as a sad, stunted zinnia, and no plant 'damps off' so quickly and easily. On the other hand, two or three seeds in a small jiffy-pot of pressed peat, thinning out to the most vigorous one, will give you magnificent upstanding plants which are very handsome and worthwhile. There are now double giant plants with frilled, quilled petals a bit like a shaggy annual aster but I still prefer the old rather thick-stemmed original variety which says 'I am a zinnia and I am not like any other flower.' They come in all colours except variations of blue and mauve, although there is an attractive plum-coloured one offered by Dobie's in their Peter Pan hybrids.

Biennials include BELLIS (the double daisy used in spring bedding schemes); Border CARNATIONS and DIANTHUS; CANTERBURY BELLS; CHEIRANTHUS (the Siberian Wallflower); FOXGLOVES (with the recent 'Excelsior' strains where the 'gloves' are spaced all round the stem so the plant faces all ways at once); HONESTY (with the silver seeds for flower arrangements and the mauve flowers in spring); *Meconopsis baileyi* is often listed as a hardy perennial, but like all true biennials once it has flowered it will it give up the ghost, and an out of this world blue poppy ghost it is! MYOSOTIS (which is the posh word for Forget-Me-Not) is the loveliest of spring foils for Darwin tulips.

I treat PANSIES as biennials, sowing them in the summer and cruelly throwing them away when they become straggly with exhaustion, after they have so generously bloomed themselves to death for us. Treat VIOLAS in the same way as pansies. *Viola cornuta* 'Alba' is a much loved plant of Christopher Lloyd's, who uses it a great deal at Great Dixter. He says it particularly likes the heavy soil of our locality, and has a six months' long season. It also has a very pleasant habit of growing into and through other plants.

Pentstemons we have talked about. The double BROMPTON STOCK should be sown mid-summer for the next year's blooming, but you must winter your plants in a frost-proof frame. SWEET WILLIAM is a biennial but it will live on for many seasons without becoming too tattered. The *Verbascum bombyciferum* is a biennial, and the first year if planted or sown in its permanent quarters will supply you with grey-frosted leaves of great size and interest before it flowers next year.

WALLFLOWERS you sow in May and June; you then thin out and plant the seedlings out separately in rows in the kitchen garden 6 in. apart, pricking out the centre of the plants to make them bushy. Then when the dahlias have succumbed to frost you transplant the wallflowers to their final quarters to flower the next spring, and to delight you with their unforgettable spring-like fragrance.

17 The Rose Garden

My best advice to you when contemplating the making of a rose garden is—before you look at your soil, your aspect or even the size of your pocket—to join the Royal National Rose Society! Then visit the Society's gardens in June and July at St Albans. Go to the shows at the Royal Horticultural Hall. Visit your nearest Provincial Display Garden and when you are in London in June go to see Queen Mary's Rose Garden in Regent's Park. Having done all this you will know more about roses than I do, so you can skip this chapter!

Consider a moment the hybrid tea and floribunda roses. They are incredibly cheap and even with inflation as it is, have risen very little in price. They will last in good, full blooming order for ten years—longer in some cases. They do not need staking. In the case of some floribundas they flower for four months continuously—even the HTs repeat themselves these days at least three times in a season. They need manure. They need pruning. They are very sturdy items in a garden 'plagued' with dogs or children. They come in every colour except blue. Their diseases are few. Tell me of another shrub or plant that has all these admirable attributes. Add to these the fact that there are fanatical rose breeders all over the world improving roses all the time and giving added fascination to your hobby by producing new varieties every year. There is always something different in the pipe-line.

So naturally in these days of labour-saving gardens a rose garden is a must. You don't just buy: you invest.

I am going to suggest a very simple design. I am going to suggest that you have an area with rustic panels round it to be the supports for the climbing and rambler rose and in front of this there will be four borders surrounding a square and then a square area, or expanse of lawn with rose beds cut out of it. In the centre will be a sundial or a pond with a fountain, or a well-head—some kind of gardening feature. When I say square, it could be a circle, or oval or rhomboid but I feel it needs to be regular in shape. And if you need to cut off this rose garden from the rest of the garden—what is wrong with a rose hedge? In these beds, symmetrical, forming a pattern round the sundial, you will have your hybrid tea roses.

The soil should be dug to a depth of 18 in., mixing in a liberal supply of well rotted manure, compost or rotted turves with the soil in which the roots will be planted. If you are planting new roses in an old rose bed you should remove at least the top 10 in. of soil and work into the sub-soil some good rotted humus and put new soil from another part of the garden on top. You can plant roses from October in open weather until March. Do no let the roots dry out in sun and wind, and do not use fresh manure anywhere near the roots when planted.

When planting, the roses should be in the ground deeply enough for the 'grafting' unions to be just below the surface of the soil. Hard prune them in the spring. Tread hard to firm the soil at planting and again at pruning time. Standard roses should be staked at planting time—climbers and ramblers should be tied to their supports immediately on planting to avoid damage from winter gales. Do not plant in wet, puddly soil or your rose bush will literally drown. If the roses arrive in very wet weather keep them in a frost-proof place covered with a heap of damp peat and a damp sack until the weather allows for planting.

There are many schools of thought about pruning. I do mine in two stages. In the autumn—quite late (early November if necessary)—I go round and remove the vigorous late growth, i.e. the softish wood which has not had time to ripen, at the same time shortening the remaining wood by one-third. This ensures that the wind will not damage or 'rock' the bush during the winter when quite large open spaces can be made round the base of the plant letting in cold rain and air. Complete the pruning in March, good hard pruning which keeps the plant a better shape and promotes good blooms and growth throughout the year. If you want a good crop of early blooms for any reason then make the second pruning a light one.

Floribundas need lighter pruning. Climbers and ramblers need no pruning at all the first year and in the following years you take out a lot of the old wood and leave the vigorous new stuff which you tie back.

Remove all suckers—these come from the root stock and are easily recognisable, their leaves being different, usually a lighter greener colour; if you allow them to grow they will eventually take over the whole plant and you will have a briar rose and not the Hybrid Tea which you bought from the nursery.

General cultivation in the season entails digging in a good mulch of rotted manure or compost and keeping down all weeds. Don't ever dig deeply round the roses as it disturbs the roots.

A healthy, well-fed tree on well drained soil should not be subject to disease. Here are the usual bug-bears:

1. *Black-spot*. If you live in a town where the air is polluted you won't get this. If you live in the country or by the sea you may. Mulch heavily with 3 in. of grass cuttings through the season and you may not get it. The spores come from the air and the ground. You may have to spray at intervals and if you had black-spot one season then you should start to spray early the next year on a regular three weekly basis.

2. *Mildew*. Some roses are subject to this more than others. The dark red fragrant ones seem to be the worst offenders. Spray at the same time as for black-spot.

3. *Rust*. I don't know about this as I've never had it, but there are good sprays such as Maneb.

Now for some suggested varieties. Do not choose your varieties from blooms you see at flower shows. Choose them from seeing beds of the various HT shrubs in public gardens, Bone Hill, or Regent's Park. As I have already mentioned, I only have roses which are fragrant, and suggest you should do the same.

Deep red: 'Papa Meilland'. Large blooms of deep red velvety crimson Marvellously fragrant and always in bloom.

'Josephine Bruce' is another dark fragrant red, but the bush is smaller and shorter and more spreading.

Bright red scarlet: 'Ernest H. Morse.' The blooms are large turkey-red and very fragrant, and are beautifully formed.

'Alec's Red.' A bright crimson, well-formed and very fragrant.

You will notice I am giving you two of each colour to choose from when I can.

Bright vermilion: 'Duke of Windsor'. This is described in the catalogues as a luminous orange. It is certainly luminous but to my mind is an intense vermilion. There is no yellow in it and there is in an orange. It has lovely dark foliage, is fragrant, and has a very barbarically thorned wood!

151

'Super Star' has a better-shaped flower than the above, and not so intense a colour. Fragrant. It is taller than the 'Duke of Windsor'. 'Super Star' is called 'Tropicana' in America and is rather like a sea-washed coral steeped in tropical sunshine.

Then there is a sort of *tan shade* much sought after and very fashionable today. I like this colour in the house more than the garden and if you want a really smashing flower arrangement use 'Bettina' and that wonderful blue-mauve-cum-maroon sweet pea called 'Olive Dunn'. Just the two flowers and the two colours—there is a magic about them when arranged together.

'Bettina.' The catalogues call it orange-flushed red and veined with bronze. It is a bright tan to me and is very subject to black-spot.

'Whisky Mac.' The same kind of colour as above, the name is indicative of its colour—it is also fragrant.

The *whites* are important as a foil and as a break between two clashing colours.

'Pascali' is the best white HT rose—it is beautiful in shape and perfume; a lovely rose. If you care to split hairs and say the next rose is not white I will have to agree with you. It is an exquisite white flushed with pink. It is a large, statuesque rose called 'Royal Highness'. It is all but white. 'Frau Karl Druschki' is a pure wax white, but it's tallish and will not look right in a bed. It is really a Hybrid Perpetual—an old stager, but obviously good to have remained so long. 'Virgo' is another white.

For a *dark pink* rose—or a cerise rose might describe her better—I recommend 'Wendy Cussons'. She smells deliciously, flowers continuously, and has a lovely shape. Another good pink is 'Prima Ballerina'—it is very fragrant and never stops blooming for me. Rosy-pink, very good for not getting black-spot. 'Mischief' is supposed to be coral-salmon—but I think it is a little more to the pink side than that; it is very fragrant and a good shape.

'Fragrant Cloud' must not be left out whilst we are talking of pinks. It is coral-pink and is beautifully fragrant as its name suggests.

For a *bi-colour* I suggest two: 'Piccadilly'—the buds are bright scarlet on the inside and gold on the outside. 'Chicago Peace' has soft pink blooms with a yellow edge. It is a sport from the famous 'Peace'. It is not terribly fragrant—but enough for me to include it!

'Blue Moon' is a rose I would have for its perfume alone;

it is soft *lilac*, a lovely colour and is fairly robust for this colour range.

All *yellow* roses—and from them all the oranges and vermilions too—come from 'Soleil d'or', first introduced to the public in 1898. A Frenchman Pernet Ducher, having spent years trying to create a yellow hybrid tea-type rose gave it up, but walking one day through his neglected rose fields found a self-sown seedling with double orange-yellow flowers. I love to try and picture this moment. It must be a little like waiting for the football results and holding the coupon in your shaky excited hand. You have nearly done—your forecast is correct except the last result to come. It comes! You are 100% correct. You throw your hat into the air, possibly your wife's as well—you have after years of toil, quite by accident come across your fortune! Your yellow rose!

'Grandpa Dickson' is one of the best yellows—a lovely shape with pointed petals. 'King's Ransom' is *the* yellow, it is always blooming and is fragrant.

From these twenty-one roses you can pick a dozen—shall we say a dozen in each bed. This way you will have a mass of each colour all blooming at the same time. A really beautiful sight. You should try to have dark red, red, tan, mauve, pink, vermilion/coral pink, bi-colour, white, yellow, thus covering the complete spectrum.

I will advise you now, if I may, of some floribundas to put in the surrounding borders amongst the species and old-fashioned roses.

'Allgold' is yellow, 'China Town' is deep yellow. 'Iceberg' is white, and is a magnificent shrub to have anywhere in the garden. 'Masquerade' is yellow, salmon-pink and scarlet all at the same time, fading to a deep rose with almost a touch of lilac. 'Lilac Charm' is mauve. The 'Queen Elizabeth' is a soft rosy-pink and is very tall. The blooms of 'Elizabeth of Glamis' are salmon-pink and the bush is not quite as tall as 'Queen Elizabeth'. 'City of Belfast' is bright orange-scarlet. 'Copper Pot' describes itself. 'Evelyn Fison' is vivid red. 'Rumba' has large trusses of yellow flowers flecked and edged with bright red.

For climbing roses let us consider first the climbers which are recurrent flowerers. 'Dance de Feu' is orange red and flowers constantly, but it hardly smells at all—sorry! 'Mermaid' is a single yellow—very beautiful. 'Parkdirector Riggers' is a dark single red. 'Pink Perpetué' has full double blooms which are fragrant. 'Casino' is a semi-double soft yellow. 'Handel' is an ivory-rose with deep pink shading looking rather like a begonia!

'Galway Bay' is pink and has blooms like a Hybrid Tea and so has 'Schoolgirl' which is apricot to soft salmon. 'Zephyrine Drouhin' is silvery-pink.

Then come the climbers and ramblers and Wichuraianas: 'Alberic Barbier' is creamy-white shaded yellow. 'Albertine', one of the greatest and most popular of all climbing roses, has reddish salmon buds opening to pale pink. 'American Pillar' has large trusses of single pink blooms with a white centre—not really fragrant. 'Emily Gray', yellow with evergreen coppery foliage. 'Gloire de Dijon' has double golden buff flowers. 'Paul's Scarlet Climber' has clusters of large red semi-double flowers of crimson scarlet. 'Paul's Lemon Pillar' has large double scented flowers of sulphur yellow.

Then there are various climbing sports which are exactly like their parents only they aspire to greater heights. One to avoid is 'Climbing Peace' as it hardly ever flowers. I had one on a south wall once which grew and grew for three years until it covered a very large part of the house, but it never ever flowered. So I sold the house.

Do not let us forget the species rose *Filipes*—the vigorously rampant white climber we last met in the white Garden at Sissinghurst. The very vigorous clone Vita Sackville-West used was *F. kiftsgate*. And it is sweetly scented.

When making a rose garden near the house it is advisable to study the exact colour of the house. Is it grey stone? Is it Snowcem white? Is it a nasty shade of brick red? Or a lovely shade of old brick! For depending on the shade of the house you will have not only to decide on the climbing roses on it, but on the colours of the roses in the beds nearest to it. A white rose on a white house is lost. A dark red rose on a pale pink house is lovely.

So there, roughly in a few pages, is your rose garden. The possibilities are infinite. But remember, if you have made your rose garden and it is complete, you can always pop the odd roses in here and there elsewhere in the garden and shrubbery. The Hybrid Teas are the most difficult to place, other than with each other in a bed or a rose garden on their own. It is an exciting exercise making a rose garden, and I wish you well with it—and I wish I were making it with you.

With new roses being invented and cultivated and sold to us with all the pressures of the modern salesman, it is quite possible, indeed more than likely, that all the Hybrid Tea roses mentioned above will be as outmoded as the dodo by the time the printers' ink is dry.

18 The Heather Garden

Do not, I implore you, make your heather garden in some corner which you think will do because you can think of nothing else to put there, and which is out of sight. Feature your heather garden, and make it solely a heather garden, with the odd dwarf conifer here and there. I made the mistake of trying to mix camellias and heather and they do not! As neither of them move well I'm stuck with them spoiling each other. Might I suggest that, as well as the odd dwarf conifer here and there you might use a few brooms and gorse, especially *Genista hispanica, Cytisus praecox, C. prostrata*, dwarf rhododendrons and *Berberis thunbergii*.

Give your heather garden a place in full sun, heathers do not need shelter from wind or snow or anything the climate can throw at them. Remember they come from the high cliffs and windy moors. Another good reason for giving your heather garden prominence, is that some of the heathers are in flower for the whole year round. No other race of plants comes easily to mind which will produce flowers throughout the year (providing they are grown in variety) and need so little attention—except for weeding and one trimming over a year, usually in the spring. 'Weeding?' you say. 'I thought that heathers were used as weed smotherers?' Well, they are, when you have had them a year or so and they have grown into each other, but you do have to make sure that they are not overwhelmed at first. It is best to buy your heather young, as larger plants do not transplant easily, and best to get them in jiffy pots so that there is little disturbance. There are so many kinds that it is a temptation to become a heather collector and see how many species and varieties you can grow. They grow from 3 in. high to 5–6 ft. with the so-called tree heathers.

There are few gardens which cannot grow heathers—for some varieties will grow in moderate lime and be quite happy. All the *carneas* will, and the Mediterranean varieties, also the hybrid *Darleyensis* 'G. Rendall' and *D. stricta*. Naturally, an acid peaty soil is their proper habitat.

The site you have chosen should be well dug and cultivated to a fine tilth, with peat and leafmould dug well in, especially if your soil is not light. Plant the shrubs (for they are really miniature shrubs) deeply and firmly into the soil from October to March—with jiffy pots at almost anytime, so long as you keep them well watered. It is best to plant them in groups of not less than three, at a foot apart. Trimming is done once a year about the middle of March—all you do is trim off the dead flowers and some of the stalk, but never very much, or you will kill them. Winter flowering sorts should be trimmed after flowering, too. This keeps the plants from becoming leggy— and they will form compact cushions which eventually join up and make a weed-impervious bed.

The tree heathers are best placed in the middle of an island bed, or at the back if your heather garden is a border, backed by a fence or hedge. *Erica arborea* has pale green feathery foliage, white scented flowers in early spring and grows to 4 ft. *E. a.* 'Alpina' is similar, up to 6 ft., and is very hardy. *E. australis* has bright pink flowers, 5–6 ft. *Erica hybrida lusitanica* (Codonodes) flowers from December to April with pink buds, white flowers and grows to 6 ft. *E. h. l.* 'Veitchii' is sweetly scented with white flowers in April and May, at 5–6 ft.

In the months after Christmas, just when we need flowers most, the gallant *carnea* heathers bring colour—and, as I have said, they do not mind a little lime. *Erica carnea* is pink, 6 in. high and flowers from December to April. *E. c.* 'Aurea', as you would expect, has gold foliage—very bright in spring and summer. The flowers are pink at 9 in. during February, March and April. *E. c.* 'Heathwood' has dark pink foliage with rosy purple flowers at 9 in. during February to April. *E. c.* 'King George' is a famous heather, deep rosy pink, 6 in., and flowers from January to April. 'Queen Mary' is pink. *E. c.* 'Praecox Rubra' is an early deep red, from November to March, at 6 in. *E. c.* 'Springwood White' is wonderfully free-flowering with large white flowers, sometimes as white as the snow it so gallantly grows through in February, March and April. 'Springwood Pink' is similar but pink. *E. c.* 'White Glow' is a paler foliaged heather, bushy with white flowers.

The Dorset heaths are the *Ciliaris* varieties which flower in July until September and October. *E. ciliaris* 'Globosa' has pink flowers and grey-green foliage 18 in. high, and blooms from July to October. *E. c.* 'Roundifolia' is pink on grey-green foliage at 1 ft., from July to October. *E. c.* 'Stoborough' is white at 18 in. July to September.

The *Cinerea* varieties are the summer-flowering heathers who dislike lime at all costs. But they do like sun. They start flowering in June, go on until September, some into October. *Erica cinerea* 'Apple Blossom' has white flowers edged with pale pink, is 1 ft. high and blooms from June to October. *E. c.* 'Atropurpurea' is a bright purple compact plant which blooms from June to September and is 8 in. high. *E. c.* 'Atrorubens' is red, and 9 in. high. *E. c.* 'Coccinea' is very dwarf with intense dark crimson flowers, 4 in. (good for the rockery, as already advised), and flowers from June to September. *E. c.* 'Hookstone Lavender' and *E. c.* 'Hookstone White' have long spikes of flowers, 9 in. high, from June to October. *E. c.* 'John Eason' has copper foliage, 1 ft. high, with deep pink flowers from June to September. *E. c.* 'Rosea Knaphill' variety has deep rose-pink flowers freely produced, 6 in., from June to October. *E. c.* 'Velvet Night' has very dark red flowers, 1 ft., June to September.

Erica hybrida darleyensis is early in December with purple-rose flowers, 18 in. high and goes on to April. *E. h. d.* 'Rubra' has mauve-purple flowers from February to April.

The Mediterranean varieties flower in the early spring and are bushy, upright and fairly tall. *E. m.* 'Hibernica' (syn, *glauca*) is pale pink, grows 3–4 ft. high and flowers in March and April. *E. m. c.* 'Alba' is white, free flowering and 2 ft. *E.m. h.* 'Rosea' is 2 ft. and a clear pink. *E. m. h.* 'Silver Beads' is a white flowering, low growing, 18 in. heather, and flowers from January to April.

The *Tetralix* varieties are good for the pond-side but do not mind ordinary conditions either. They flower from June to September. *Erica tetralix* 'Darleyensis' is salmon pink at 6 in. and *E. t.* 'Ken Underwood' has large cerise flowers at 1 ft.

Erica vagans—the Cornish heath—is densely busy, covering 3–4 ft. of ground in time, and it flowers from July to August with long cylindrical spikes. *E. v.* 'Lyonesse' is pure white with chestnut anthers, is 2 ft. high and blooms from July to October. *E. vagans* 'Mrs D. F. Maxwell' is 2 ft. and has deep cherry-pink flowers. *E. v.* 'St Keverne' is 2 ft. and bright rose pink.

The Lings or Callunas need a lime-free soil and require clipping over in April. *Calluna vulgaris* 'Alba' is the White Heath of Scotland. (It's terribly unlucky for me, and gypsies get quite annoyed when I shy away and will not buy it.) *C. v.* 'Gold Haze' has brilliant orange-yellow foliage throughout the year. *C. v.*

'H. E. Beale' has 10 in. spikes of double rose-pink flowers, at 2 ft., in September and October. *C. v.* 'Serlei Aurea' is a golden variety which retains the colour of its foliage throughout the year, and has white flowers 18 in. high which bloom in August and September.

I propagate heathers in late September by taking cuttings about 2 in. long. I remove the leaves of the bottom one inch and insert most of these round the edges of pots of half sand and half leafmould, or John Innes compost. Then I water well and cover the pot with a polythene bag which is firmly held in an air-tight grip by an elastic band round the edge of the pot. In six weeks' time these leaves will have rooted. I then transplant in a seed tray of potting compost, or each one goes into a jiffy pot—the smallest one—of compost and is kept in a shady frame and watered carefully. In the spring following, I plant out in the open with every hope of success. The tree heathers are difficult but the others are as easy as lavender!

You will get very attached to your heather garden. When it is fully grown it needs so little attention and as it flowers all the year round it is always interesting. Some of the very dwarf kinds can be enlivened in season with scillas, crocuses and snowdrops planted amongst them.

19 The Iris Garden

If you must have an individual garden, a rose garden is the first priority—with an iris garden as your second choice. Iris do grow well in a mixed border, given good drainage and sun, and their leaves are a good contrast to round-leaved and dumpy plants; but there is nothing so beautiful in June as a small garden devoted entirely to irises.

The colour range of the modern bearded iris is almost unbelievable. Blue: 'Foamy Wave' is a deep sky blue iris with white ruffing at the base of the standards. I had better explain; the 'standard' is the tall upright middle part of the bloom, and the 'falls' are the side petals which gracefully fall downwards on four sides. Blue is, I suppose, the colour one usually associates with the iris—certainly if one is past middle-age, since in one's youth most irises were blue. From blue to mauve: 'Allegiance' is a fine dark mauve-blue with the 'beard' (this is the centre, as it were, of the falling side petal) tipped with lemon. For a navy-blue fall and a dark violet-purple standard try 'Royal Torch'. 'Wabash' has white standards with ultramarine falls. The 'Cliffs of Dover' is pure white, large, loosely ruffled and a great one for increasing its rhizomes.

An expensive but exotic delicate white with dainty web-like stitching of rosy heliotrope round the margins of both falls and standard, is 'Rosy Veil'. 'Blue Shimmer' is sparkling white with an all-over pattern of clear blue stippling and is large, full and cheaper. 'Sable Night' is rich black-velvet with an undertone of claret, and is as dark an iris as I would want to own. 'Lavanesque' is lavender-pink; 'Royal Tapestry' is red with a purple shade, and a touch of bronze about it. 'Buttermere' is bright yellow and vigorous. 'Brazilia' is a brilliant shade of henna brown. 'Wild Ginger' has standards of warm gingery-brown with creamy-white falls, flushed and stippled with the same shade of brown. 'Brave Show' has brilliant yellow standards and maroon falls with a yellow beard. 'Happy Birthday' is flamingo pink. 'Lady Ilse' is a perfect foil for 'Happy Birthday', she is powder blue with a silver cast and an overall glistening sheen. 'Celestial Glory' is orange-yellow and tan. 'Genevieve' is a strong grower with cream standards and lemon-yellow falls. And so I could go on and on—that is why there is an Iris Society and nurserymen who specialise only in the breeding, selling and importing of irises. It is a glorious flower; it comes at the height of summer—in June—when the garden is at its most exciting. And it is so easy to grow.

Iris do well even on poor soils—but they must have a position in full sun and a well-drained site with some lime. There are some who say do not bury the rhizome—leave this above the soil to take in the sun, and I now quote from the catalogue of possibly the most important seller and breeder of iris who says: 'The rhizomes should be planted just below the surface of the ground at a depth of 1–1½ in., spreading the roots; this is facilitated if a slight mound is made. Firm the soil around the rhizome and water well to settle the soil if conditions are dry.'

I must say this sounds the easier way, as leaving the rhizome above the ground whilst settling the long wiry roots in the ground around, is a ticklish business. I do like to see the rhizomes of my iris basking in the sun, but having read the above in so distinguished a catalogue, I am inclined to rush out into the garden and put all my rhizomes to bed. In any case the theory is, amongst the old gardening fraternity, that the iris rhizome will work its way up to the surface and the *plant will not flower until it has done so*. I do hope I've stirred up a bit of controversy—but I'd like to have settled the argument to help you. Go and get yourself two pennyworth of mixed irises and try both ways!

The best time for planting seems to be August to November —if you plant in the spring, in March (and you may do so), you will not have a proper blooming season that same summer, as they do not have sufficient time to get established.

They need to be dug up and separated every third or fourth year, depending on the vigour of the variety, and do this as soon as possible after flowering. You discard the old middle portions of the clumps and replant the vigorous outside fans.

As the iris roots very near to the surface you must be very careful when weeding and forking amongst them. No manure is required, but when you are separating and digging up, renew the soil in the bed so that it does not get sour and too depleted. Provide a little dry powdery compost in the spring— or the tiniest dressing of bone manure. Any excess of nitrogen will cause the plant to have too much foliage, too little flower and will make the plant susceptible to all sorts of diseases. You should remove the outer leaves as they die, especially after flowering—a smart tug is better than cutting, but you should cut the flower stem as near to the base of the plant as possible (without damaging the leaves) when the flower has died. Plant 2 ft. apart. It is good to plant three rhizomes of one kind about 8 in. apart in a triangle with the fan of the leaves at the corners. As the foliage dies down in the autumn it should be burnt to prevent disease spreading. On heavy soils irises do best on a raised bed with the addition of plenty of leaf-mould and sand to the soil. A dry wall of two or three courses of manufactured stone (without any cement), so that the soil will drain well, is admirable in damp soils, and looks very well with the grey of the stone complementing the grey-green of the leaves. Iris do not need staking, but they are not partial to a windy site.

To prolong the season of an iris garden it is a good idea to have an edging of dwarf lavender round the beds which will flower when the irises are over, and it is also possible, with the foliage so similar, to plant between the rhizomes in late March and early April, bulbs of gladioli which will then flower later in the season. (Incidentally a species kind of gladioli, *G. byzantinus*, a rich wine colour, planted amongst *Nepeta mussini* is a glorious summer sight). Put a little sand under the bulb as you plant your gladioli; it prevents rot and helps the bulb to root well. You should feed gladioli well with copious draughts of liquid manure to get properly magnificent blooms but you will not be allowed to do this amongst the iris, as iris do not need to be watered unless it is drought weather, and they do not want to be fed, as explained above. So the gladioli in the iris garden will have a poor time of it, but you can take special care of them the following year by planting them elsewhere and pampering them. Take care when you lift your gladioli—when the leaves have died down; try not to break off the leaves at the neck of the bulb as this prevents them flowering well next year. When dry and the tops have properly died off—you leave them to dry in a seed box in a window or in the cold greenhouse. Put the bulbs in an old net bag, the sort we used to use for tennis balls, and hang them from the potting shed roof (frost-proof of course) for the winter and thwart the mice. I would rather be a mice-thwarter than break their silken backs in traps. If you thwart them enough they will go next door.

When you take the gladioli out of the ground you will find

that they are surrounded by many tiny bulbs or bulblets. These you must collect and keep till the following May. Then make a drill in the kitchen garden—with a sandy base to it—sow your bulblets and in two years you will have enriched yourself with several hundreds of gladioli bulbs. They will come true to variety, and impoverish your usual supplier, as you will not need any more gladioli bulbs from him.

For edging your iris garden there is an attractive race of vigorous hybrid iris producing perfectly formed iris flowers, in miniature. They can also be used to advantage in the rock garden—they flower earlier than the tall bearded varieties—and they are fragrant. So if you use these in the iris garden you will be prolonging your flowering period. It is wrong, I think, to use the Dutch and Spanish iris in conjunction with the bearded iris in an iris garden. This is only my opinion, for what it is worth. They are such different looking flowers that they detract from each other.

Whilst we are talking of iris, I must mention *Iris reticulata*. Here is a worthwhile wrinkle about the small flower which so gallantly flowers in January—dig some up and bake them in the sun in July and August in your greenhouse, and then put them back again in the garden. They will make an even braver and earlier show.

20 Exotics and Oddities

'Is your book for the sophisticated gardener?' said one Luncheon Club lady when I told her what I was up to. My reply was that I didn't think it was. 'I mention some quite rare shrubs and plants,' I said, 'and I also have to tell the beginners how to lay a path and hoe a row.' 'Oh,' she said. 'In that case I shall not buy it!' Some of those of you who have come this far with me will have done so because you are keen to know a little more, and some because you want to be reminded of gardening items and procedures you have missed or forgotten about. I can well understand the sophisticated plantsman and very knowledgeable gardener not wanting to be told of 'London Pride' or of 'Mrs Sinkins' pinks, or how to take a hard-wood cutting. I once browsed through some gardening books upstairs at Hatchards in Piccadilly next to Michael Caine, the famous film actor, and I think we were both amused at the amount we knew and did not know about gardening. 'I read every gardening book that comes out,' he said.

But no matter how experienced a gardener, we all have fun, and the following are a few oddities just jotted down for your amusement. If you don't already grow them, do try, because they are always a good talking point when you show someone around, or at your luncheon table when you are entertaining and the odd dish arrives (on the table, not a guest!).

The ORNAMENTAL GOURD. These are grown on trellis or pea sticks or allowed to wander down a dry bank. The gourds are like quaintly shaped melons, pumpkins or marrows, with graphic names like 'Calabash', 'Caveman's Club' and 'Turk's Turban'; these are the large fruited ones. Then there are small fruited ones shaped like apples, oranges, pears, eggs, bottles and spoons. These are, of course, the fleshy covered seeds.

You dry the seeds and use them for home decoration; some are enhanced by a colourless varnish. Do not throw them on the fire when you have tired of the decoration for they will explode with a loud report like a bomb. There is a dishcloth gourd which is inedible (but who has a penchant for dishcloth eating?) and it is from this kind of gourd that the bathroom loofah is obtained.

RHUBARB CHARD has long stalks of bright crimson with deep purple leaves; these are useful for flower arrangements, but they are also fun to use as a foliage plant in the mixed border. Similarly one grows ASPARAGUS for the ferns and not for the mouth-watering shoots. RED CABBAGE is fun too for flower arrangements. So is the variegated cabbage.

PUMPKINS can be raised in pots like marrows in a greenhouse or frame, and provided you have a fairy god-mother and a few rats you will be able to arrange extra transport to take your guests home.

There is a blue COCOA-BEAN, with a deep blue pod, it has purple flowers and stems and purplish foliage. You top and tail, and eat whole like a runner-bean.

The GLOBE ARTICHOKE should be grown at the back of the mixed border. The leaves are enormous and theatrical and the flowers if allowed to continue (instead of greedily eating them) come to a magnificent thistle-like head.

The ANGELICA is a stately herb of the *Kex* family and its leaves alone are worthy of a place in the border. Its large yarrow like heads are 3–4 ft. high. You candy the stems.

There is a variegated KALE which has brilliant colours in mid-winter. It brightens up the kitchen garden in the darker days. Use it in the mixed border.

Also fun is a BUSH MARROW called 'Gold Nugget' which has rounded fruit like a miniature pumpkin, and you can store it in the winter. And 'Custard Pie', which sounds like a comedian's stock-in-trade, is another bush marrow with flattened white round fruit, 7 in. in diameter.

Another novelty, but not if you are growing commercially, is the GOLDEN OXHEART TOMATO. It is bright yellow and grows to such an enormous size that one is sufficient for a whole salad. It has an ox-heart shape and excellent flavour.

Hardly a novelty, but worth mentioning whilst we are talking about vegetables, is the French MANGE-TOUT, or sugar pea, where you eat the whole issue, pod and all, like you would a French bean. I couldn't, in fact bring myself to do so in case there was a small visiting maggot inside, of which I have a horror.

HAMBURG PARSLEY is grown for its roots which are like large white carrots and, grated raw, taste like nuts. And here is a quaintness for those who think that Queen Bee Jelly gives

you a longer life and a more worthwhile one; this is GREEK
PARSLEY which contains Apiol, the same mystic substance.

Are you shy? Would you like to share your shyness with
Mimosa pudica—the sensitive pot plant which has wonderfully
ornamental foliage which shrinks and folds up when touched.
If you are keen on a nervous breakdown get some *Briza Maxima*
or *B. minima* at the same time; its other name is Quaking
Grass.

The BALLOON VINE (*Cardiospernum halicacabum*) is a half-
hardy annual which quickly climbs to 10 ft. and has small white
flowers which mature into large spherical fruits. It comes from
Bermuda.

Have you tried all these?

21 The Secret Garden

I have explained to you how surprise is important when you are planning a garden, and how it is desirable that you should not be able to see it all at once. This is difficult if your garden is small, but even then you can so design it that a path leads your eye on, as if it goes somewhere. The fact that when you actually walk round the corner where the path has taken you, to find you are slap up against the next door neighbour's fence, does not matter, if the path leads your eye that way in the design from a distance. If you have a small enclosure at this point, consisting of a 7 ft. high hedge (yew or purple beech or *Cupressus lawsonia*) it might be fun to have a circular hedge so that your enclosure could be grandly called the rotunda. Then you have found an excellent place for your secret garden.

If it is small and the hedges are high there will not be much sun in there and the hedges will take a lot of the goodness from the soil, so I suggest in this case you have a paved area with perhaps a statue in it. A paved area with a small pond and fountain is another alternative. What about having a stone seat for lovers? With an arbour of sweetly-scented climber over it: summer jasmine, honeysuckle, or that wonderful white climbing rose *Felipes kiftsgate*.

If the enclosure is slightly larger, say 15 ft. square (or in diameter if circular), you could have a little garden in there, and as it is bound to be a bit shady, make it a white garden—and certainly a very scented one. If you can make it larger still, have a seat with an arbour to watch a fountain playing over a pond.

Did you see the film or the play *The Gazebo*. If you did, you will know what I mean by a gazebo. If not, it is a 'folly' or a summer-house usually built in the Greek or Roman idiom with pillars and a cupola roof. This kind of summer-house is wonderfully atmospheric. There is a semi-circular one with a few steps up and pillars, as a commemorative building in the Dartington Hall garden. This is not a secret garden, for as you sit there a great view stretches out in front of you for miles. At

Stourhead the gazebos are grand pavilions or temples, and you see them in vistas across vast lakes looking over the shoulders of peacocks (live peacocks not topiary ones). When I think of the money left by George Bernard Shaw, and the miserable little wooden summer-house in which he wrote, in a ghastly, unimaginative, scrubby garden at his hideous house near Welwyn in Hertfordshire, I can hardly believe him to have been an artistic person at all. His way of life seemed so lacking in style whereas his writing is not.

As well as stone gazebos, there are also ones made of iron, looking in a way like little bandstands on the ends of piers, made of iron lace. They are not expensive structures and when covered with climbing shrubs are very elegant to look upon. There is white iron or aluminium garden furniture to match, which is durable, not too heavy, and also very stylish in Georgian and Victorian shapes. If you wish to re-create an old world atmosphere there are also edging hoops to match, such as I remember as a child in the parks of now out-of-date small seaside resorts in the West Country.

Inside your secret garden you could have a bird-bath—a sundial would not get enough sun. Or you could have a stone trough garden a few feet from the ground.

Lead cisterns and urns from old gardens are very costly indeed, but here would be a perfect home for them. There are some beautiful fibre glass replicas made of them today (Verine is one trade name whose products I admire), which are not cheap but excellent in their way.

If your secret garden is small then it will be shady and the ideal place for a bed of ferns. These will need ample humus and the shade will be ideal. *Adiantum venustum* is the delicate-looking but hardy Maidenhair fern. *Athyrium filix-foemina* is the Lady Fern—with divided fronds and a lacy look, described as a graceful shuttlecock. The Male Buckler fern is the *Dryopteris filix-mas*, rising to 3½ ft., good for dry shade and is in good foliage from May to September. For a giant, use *Osmunda regalis,* but he needs a moist position. Very much to my regret he failed in my dry woodland soil and instead of a giant I had a very miserable pigmy. The Hart's Tongue ferns will spread everywhere, but what could be nicer! *Phyllitis scolopendrium* is their correct name and when they are really at home with you, you will find them in the crevices of steps and dry stone walls. They are welcome wanderers, for it is things like this which give your garden the mature look. *P. s.* 'Undulatum' has leaves with waved margins and this is the one I have, having transplanted it from a bank in one of my fields. The spleen-worts also established themselves in old walls and steps and are most attractive, especially the black spleenwort *Asplenium adiantum* 'Nigrum'.

You want to contrive your secret garden so that it is different from the rest—a 'casket' containing something precious. I think I prefer a statue in mine, some garden god that I can commune with.

22 The Woodland Garden

Here hills and vales, the woodland and the plain,
Here earth and water seem to strive again;
Not chaos-like together crushed and bruised,
But, as the world, harmoniously confused:
Where order in variety we see,
And where, though all things differ, all agree.
Here waving groves a chequered scene display
And part admit, and part exclude, the day . . .
There interspersed in lawns and opening glades
Thin trees arise that shun each other's shades.
Here in full light the russet plains extend:
There wrapped in clouds the blueish hills ascend.
Ev'n the wild heath displays her purple dyes,
And midst the desert fruitful fields arise.

Alexander Pope

Have you a wood? If you have not you can skip this chapter
as it is a difficult task to create a woodland of your own in a
lifetime. Beverley Nichols started one once in his first garden
when he was very young, and its story makes one of the fun-
niest chapters in his first gardening book, *Down the Garden Path*!
I suppose you could create something a little wood-like in a
few years, using very quick-growing trees as explained in my
chapter on speed. 'A woodland garden', says Francis Bacon, 'is
to be framed as much as may be to a natural wilderness.' It
must be tamed but it must not appear so. A haphazard exu-
berence has been thought out in detail. And because a garden
is a manufactured picture with colours and pigments, canvas
and frames gathered from all over the world, your wood will
be a nightmare of unnaturalness. Trees from Chile and China together, wreathed in climbers from England and Japan and
carpeted with flowers from Turkey and Italy and Spain and
North America. If only the nations of the world would live
as happily and harmoniously as do the plants of a garden.

You will try to have flowers right through the year. You will endeavour with foliage plants to have as much variety of foliage to look at through the year as possible, but do remember here that the golden plants and shrubs show but little of their splendour in the shade—they revert to a sickly green. There will be good cover, medium-sized shrubs, small trees, forest trees and there will be climbers and trailers in the trees. Also you will create, if you can, little vistas and views through your wood which are enhanced at various seasons with different plants.

There is no reason why you should not plant an avenue of trees to take you to your wood. You may not live to enjoy it yourself but it is a way of becoming famous, if only locally. Someone has to start an avenue so why not you? If you are a bit half-hearted, consider an avenue of smaller trees such as cherries or laburnums or a pleached avenue of limes, or hornbeams. This would give your garden a very French look.

The following suggestions will not make a wood—but in a small garden they can give the impression of a wood—and a very floriferous one at that. Remember all these are small trees and not recommended for strolling amongst by very tall men! *Prunus* (Flowering Cherry) of many kinds, 'Kanzan', 'Miyako', *P. Serrulata* 'Grandiflora', 'Yukon' (the pale primrose-yellow/green), *P. sargentii*. The double pink thorn *Crataegus oxyacantha* 'Rosea Plena'. *Robinia hillieri*—do choose several robinias; they are so delicate and beautiful. A novelty like the Handkerchief Tree, *Davidia involucrata* 'Vilmoriniana'. Various maples, particularly *Acer negundo* 'Variegatum' to give a sunny effect—put it near a purple leaved prunus. The sweet Gum *Liquidambar styraciflua*, The Maidenhair Tree *Ginkgo biloba*. The Mountain Ash (*Sorbus aucuparia*) and *Sorbus hupehensis* with white berries. Some crab apples would give flower and fruit for decoration: *Malus* 'Profusion', *M. floribunda* and, on the edge of the wood, the Weeping Birch, *Betula pendula* 'Youngii'. *Amelanchier*—the Snowy Mespilus. And *Mespilus germanica*, the Medlar. *Cotinus coggygria* 'Atropurpureus' (the Smoke Bush) is generally thought of as a shrub, but there is one on the A272 road to the east of Haywards Heath which must be all of 20 ft. high and I drive dangerously with envy as I pass it. Whilst we are thinking of purple—do plant a *Fagus sylvatica* 'Purpurea', the Copper Beech.

Ilex aquifolium, the common holly, is quicker growing than you think, and there are various variegated kinds, notably 'Silver Queen' and Golden King' which are slower growing.

Laburnum is about the right size for this tiny wood, so is the Sumach—or *Rhus glabra*.

I wonder if a Weeping Willow would be right, on the edge of the wood, a little to one side as you entered it. It would grow quickly and give the others shelter and give you encouragement. So would a few Lombardy poplars, balsam poplars and silver-leaved poplars, all mentioned before.

There must be some conifers in your tiny wood. These will give it 'body' in the winter and shelter, too. But you must place them well—a group of three contrasting ones here and there. Use them to form the dark, mysterious background of the wood—*leylandii* would be very useful here.

Cedrus atlantica 'Glauca' will grow to 40 ft. but not, madam, in your time. *Chamaecyparis lawsoniana* 'Lanei' (golden), *C. l.* 'Lutea', *Abies concolor* (a fir tree). *Cryptomeria japonica* 'Elegans' has feathery foliage and makes a small tree. *Cupressus macrocarpa* 'Gold Crest' will grow quickly, but it must be on the sunny side of the wood.

When planting your wood you should position your trees in groups of three here, four or five there, with vistas arranged between them to make a design and to arrange shafts of sunlight and, of course, to conform to some kind of path or progress which you will make through the wood. If the wood is already there, then you must thin it sufficiently to allow planting of shrubs, and also to allow for a progress through the wood.

I think it would now be helpful to give a short list of some shrubs which are suitable for shade. That is to say, shrubs to use amongst your trees in the woodland garden: andromeda, arundinaria, buxus, *Camellia japonica* and *C. williamsii*, *Cornus canadensis* and *C. alba* 'Elegantissima', daphne, elaeagnus, euonymus, *Fatsia japonica*, fuchsia, hypericum, some hydrangeas ilex, kerria, *Mahonia aquifolium*, pieris, rhododendrons (hardy hybrids and *ponticum*), azaleas, *Rubus tricolor*, skimmia, *Viburnum davidii*, vinca. The periwinkles and the ivies should vie with each other for ground cover.

Ferns are splendid plants for the woodland garden. Amongst them bulbs—snowdrops, scillas, muscaris, leucojums, bluebells and narcissus and daffodils, should be planted liberally.

Other bulbs for massing in the woodland garden are: aconite, anemone, chionodoxa, colchicum, crocus, ixia. Bulbs for groups in the wild garden could be: fritillaria, *Gladiolus primulinus*, *Iris pumila*, *Lilium chalcedonicum*, *L. tigrinum* 'Splendens', and montbretia. When you plant your bulbs, never put them formally in lines—it is best to shut the dogs in the house and then to throw down a handful in front of you and to plant them as they fall. This way you will get a natural informality.

Plants for the woodland garden: aconitum, lathyrus (the ever-lasting pea—this will need sun), myosotis, digitalis, lily-of-the-valley, meconopses, orchids, primroses and primulas, violets, polygonatum (Solomon's Seal), various flowering nettles.

Among the climbing plants, use ivies, clematis (where the flowers can reach the sun but the root remains in the shade), rubus, jasminum and various honeysuckles (lonicera).

23 Speed in the Garden

When one buys a house it is a comparatively quick and easy job to make the necessary additions and subtractions—indeed to build from scratch will at most take you a year—and to decorate the inside of the house perhaps three months. But outside—the garden! How long will that take? If you are as old as I am (and I'm in my sixtieth year) you will have seen trees, which were saplings straight from the nursery when planted in your youth at the sides of some of the new roads, grow to mature forest giants. What about those magnificent poplars on either side of the road as you are about ten miles from London on the A1?

Seven years ago I knocked a house down, built another on the only piece of garden that the old house had, i.e. the front lawn, and set to on making a garden as quickly as possible in the surrounding fields. I walked round first and decided that amongst my assets were some splendid beech trees—two over a hundred years old—that I could include in my garden. Some tall Scots Pines, which added little, but it would be a shame to remove them. A small wood of hazel-nut trees—very old and past their prime. Most blessed of all I was the owner of an avenue of neglected beech trees and the drive up to the house had also an avenue of trees which were decimated by storms and disease and which most regrettably have declined in numbers annually.

I am on a windy site, four hundred feet above sea level, twelve miles from the South Coast (I can see the sea twelve miles away), and I have a wife who is a determined and lovable woman who insists at all costs that the view must be preserved and no vestige of it must be lost behind trees or hedges.

The few rhododendrons in the wood and up the avenue were either *ponticums* or just did not flower. I felt I needed to replace and re-plant, being extremely fond of rhododendrons, and having an acid soil. Apart from the wind, I had an ideal site, so I studied all rhododendrons and tried hard to remember the ones I had enjoyed in previous gardens. I found, as a result of my study, that one can purchase rhododendrons which grow quickly. I made a selection of them, red, pink, mauve and yellow, all of which would grow quickly and make man-high bushes in a few years. Here they are:

White: 'Geo. Hardy' 'Sappho.'
Yellow: 'Butterfly', 'China', 'Harvest Moon'.
Red: 'Fred Waterer' and 'Grand Arab'.
Scarlet: 'J.G. Millais', 'Lamplighter', 'Garibaldi'.
Crimson: 'Cynthia' and 'Lady Longman'.
Pink: 'Corry Coster', 'Midsummer', 'Pierre Moser', 'Pink Pearl'.
Deep Pink: 'Betty Wormwald' and 'Lady Cathcart'.
Mauve: 'A. Bedford' and 'Lady Decies'.

These went in in the second year, so they are now six years old. Some are already over 6 ft. high and look very sparse and leggy. Some, like 'Pink Pearl,' which I ordered in spite of the fact that it is not a *particularly* quick grower, look magnificent at 3–4 ft. high. Some of the quick growers I placed in windy sites too near the beech trees, who took all the moisture and nutriment, and they have only grown perhaps a foot higher than when I had them. Luckily, being surface rooted, they move easily so I have found better homes for some, and they have now begun to grow properly. So be advised over rhododendrons if you are in a hurry; get some of the quicker, bigger plants for the back of your groups but do not concentrate on all of these varieties. Plants grow much more quickly than you imagine.

When you have a new garden with vast spaces to fill, you panic. I did. I deliberately over-planted so that we achieved as full, and as mature a look as possible. This I did by buying a dozen of this and a dozen of that as I saw shrubs advertised cheaply in the gardening papers. I bought a dozen *Berberis stenophylla* very cheaply, small straggly plants. They are beautiful plants now, 3 ft. wide and 5 ft. tall with plenty of suckers to make many more plants from them. Similarly, two dozen amelanchier shrubs were purchased from a woodland nursery which supplied them very cheaply as pheasant cover for woodlands. They grew very strongly and filled the spaces well. A dozen sweet briar were also bought and I have not removed a single one; I love them, and will not remove them ever. Tiny, 9 in. long single slips they were, bought as hedging plants, and now they are enormous bushes constantly being cut back. A dozen very cheap *Cydonia japonica*—chaenomeles, I should call them now—these were tiny plants about 6 in. high; they are now several feet high and are being removed to a wild garden as they are very poor quality and I try never to throw away any plant. These are not good enough quality to *give away*! I have mentioned this several times and will do so again: particularly if you have a small garden, only buy the very best. If the health of a plant which you buy is poor, it will take several seasons to restore to health, and time cannot be wasted in this way. If you purchase a poor variety it will take up as much space and require as much loving care as the best possible variety.

Buddleias, because they grew so quickly and were so rewarding, were bought in profusion. They are very cheap, too, even the best named varieties. These have seeded and I have not thrown any seedlings away, but I shall now have to, as the spaces are being filled out by choicer shrubs.

At the local market I bought a dozen un-named floribunda roses. These were cheap and in poor health, but a season's care has put them right—three of them were 'Queen Elizabeth', which is a wonder rose for quick growing and as a quick-growing screen. I prune mine allowing for height as these three are at the back of a shrub border. They are 8 ft. high, as I write, and a mass of HT-type blooms in the cheriest and dearest of pinks. Roses will establish quickly and give a good account of themselves, even in the first years.

Having several acres to fill quickly is a daunting prospect for the pocket. What shrubs grow quickly from seed? Tree lupins—these were 2 ft. high in a year and cost but a few pence for a dozen. I always have some—their scent is worth having for that alone, as well as the shape of the bushes and the colour of the flowers. Brooms grow very quickly and cheaply from seed (cytisus). Some were pink, some red, some red and yellow; all from the same packet, and although they are reckoned to be short-lived, some I have in the kitchen garden, seven years old, kept just for flower arrangements, are flourishing from this original sowing and are 10 ft. high.

Many shrubs from my old garden were brought over at once and dibbled in a shady moist spot until I could find a proper place for them as the garden evolved. No sooner were they in than I was taking layered cuttings from them into pots of sand and compost placed around them. One quite small skimmia I am very fond of produced me eight mature shrubs in three years this way—bigger than the ones I got from the nursery!

Being on a windy site, I needed quick-growing shelter. I

started hedges of *Cupressus lawsoniana*, as already explained, with deep trenches of old cow manure and leaf mould for their roots to enjoy, and they rewarded me with 15 ft. high hedges in seven years from 1½ ft. plants. *Cupressus leylandii* was used here and there as specimen plants and are now 25 ft. high. Poplars—Lombardy and scented balsam poplars grow quickly. So did one weeping willow; the other is still a sickly dwarf. Eucalyptus raced ahead to become mature trees—actual trees—in three years.

For screening, *Polygonum baldschuanicum*—the Russian Vine—covered the central-heating oil tank in a season and we are now fighting to hold it back. *Lonicera halliana* was up and over the house in two years. *Cobaea scandens*, a rare beauty, grew 15 ft. high in a year—but it is an annual. However you will have to depend on many annuals to give you your mature look in a first year. Nasturtiums are useful, too. Some of the tall grasses will help to give shelter to a struggling young hedge. This is a useful gimmick.

Ligustrum vulgare 'Aureum'—golden privet—was purchased and two dozen dotted here and there where we needed a sunny yellow; they were a cheap, useful fillers-in and very vigorous. The hypericums were cheap and quick, and with me, so were the hydrangeas, but north of the midlands they would not be quick. I was quite wicked, and picked armsful of pussy willows (*Salix caprea*) from the hedgerows and planted them here and there in the damper parts; they grew into large bushes and did their job of filling-in magnificently. They have gone now and in the spring I miss them.

If you are in a hurry the first job is to plant the hedges. Then the shrubberies, then the herbaceous plants. Trees need to be sited and planted as soon as you get your new garden. These are the items which need time. Some sycamore are quick, most poplars and all eucalyptus. The *Prunus* 'Kanzan', which Vita Sackville-West thought vulgar, is fairly quick.

A word of warning for all those in a hurry. A large shrub or tree sometimes takes several years to establish itself in a new site and by this time a young, vigorous, healthy plant (which will cost you much less) will have caught up the larger tree, and will then proceed to win the race in size and height because it is happy and at home.

A garden really establishes itself in about three years. In six it is almost mature. Plant generously, using plenty of fill-ins which you will remove later.

It is tempting to run before you can walk and, having used

all kinds of subterfuge in making my present garden as mature as possible, I can only draw attention to the one item I had resigned myself to be patient about. The yew hedge. It will take years, I said—I don't suppose I'll live to see it in its mature glory! That was only six years ago and now it is my height—no less, for I cannot see over it—I certainly cannot see through it. All I did was to give it plenty to feed on at the beginning. So there really is not any need to rush. A garden is purposefully a quiet, slow place.

24 Mistakes to Avoid

When I originally set out to write this book, I made twenty-five headings for chapters and wrote Chapter 24—Confessions of a Keen Amateur. I suppose the principal mistake I have made in a long amateur career as a gardener is to have the presumption to write a book about it. A book which for many enthusiasts and knowing gardeners will have a thousand errors and half-truths and exposures of raw ignorance. The keener one is, however, the more trial and errors one will make. There is one certainty—a gardener will reap in beauty what he gives in labour.

I have, however, mentioned many a mistake as I have gone along. Do not be in too much of a hurry, as I always have been. I had to build a dry stone wall several times because there was a spring behind it and the gathering water pushed it down—but it would not have been pushed down if I had used the largest, heaviest stones for the bottom two courses and if I had 'battered' it sufficiently.

A garden will grow much more quickly than you ever imagine. Do not always buy the quickest grower. This has been one of my mistakes. I will—also with a desire to get a well-furnished effect at once—plant too closely. This does not matter too much if you are bedding out, except that a cramped plant will never be able to show off its full beauty. However with permanent plantings it is often a disaster, and in two or three years heartbreaking decisions have to be made as to which tree or shrub to move, as one is smothering the other. This situation is caused by one's lack of imagination in visualising the future 'look' of a planting. Always err on being too far apart when planting and if things do look bare, put in a cheap, short-lived filler, like a broom or tree lupin.

When you plant a forest tree, make sure it will, all its life, have plenty of space. Think, when planting a forest tree, of its roots in relation to the foundations of your house. By the time you are paying the final instalment to the building society the roots from your 'little' wood of twenty-five years ago will be knocking your precious homestead over.

Do not hurry over the preparation of the foundations of permanent features like balustrades because you are too keen and excited to see the future effect, as I have done! You will only have to do it all over again, perhaps after a rose has clothed it with long, trailing branches full of thorns!

Do not show-off when using gardening machinery. I was once rather pleased with the way I was mowing the grass round the top of my mill pond bank when I allowed the mower to take me into the pond, thus getting me the best family laugh I've ever had.

Do not buy the very cheapest lots you see advertised sometimes, when you think 'I surely cannot get as much as that for so little money.' You won't of course. What you will get will be spindly little stuff of poor quality. But I must qualify this admonition by saying that this stuff is exactly right for filling up odd corners where in a year or so it will have reached a reasonable size. Use the cheap lot for in-filling and then throw away in years to come. I would much rather do this than have acres of bare earth.

It might be better not to make compost than to use half-rotted stuff full of weeds. Because I went into my wood and dug out several loads of leaf-mould which was full of seed, I have given myself the task of a lifetime in removing a pernicious kind of creeping sorrel. I was using this very fibrous leaf-mould to help break up my back-breaking sticky wealden clay. Peat would have helped in the same way but there are no weed seeds in peat. I am pleased, however, with the way my clay is gradually disappearing and becoming a reasonably workable soil, but you have to keep at it, and all the time add fibrous material, otherwise it tends to revert and get stickier. If you use old manure which has been stacked in a midden for some time, as I did, it is worth the bother of passing it through a sieve before you use it, then you will rid yourself of the tiny pieces of white root from twitch, convolvulus, nettle (yellow in this case) thistle and ground elder, which you might then spread over your garden and take a life-time of springs to remove. Also, when you accept an old root of an herbaceous plant from a friend, tease that root out, search it thoroughly to make sure you are not importing some of his best weeds instead. For the same reason the importation of soil into your garden will give you just as much trouble if you do not thoroughly 'go over it' before you use it.

It's a terrible mistake to put in new plants in the autumn if the ground is too wet when they arrive. Have patience; keep them damp and warm, and put them in when your ground is dry and frost-free. I lost a whole row of hedge for this reason once.

Mistakes, however, are useful. You will learn from yours as well as from mine.

25 Conclusions

George Bernard Shaw wrote 'Those who can, do; those who can't, teach.' And I think he was right. I certainly cannot teach; this I discovered once when I tried to teach the Comedy Class at The Guildhall School of Music and Drama some years ago. I resigned after two terms before I did too much damage to the pupils and too much damage to myself in realising that the craft of comedy apart from a few basic rules is something you either have or you have not. I believe this is true of all arts and the art of gardening is no exception. A methodical person who does the right thing at the right time but has no artistic flair, will have a good garden of one kind; and the artistic person who lacks the application required of method will have a garden of another kind. Let us hope, dear Reader, you are both combined. Your garden then will be a fantasia of delight.

As well as the flair and the patience and the strength and will to work you will need the garden too, and with any luck a view. John James in his book *The Theory and Practice of Gardening*, published in 1712, wrote 'The fourth thing required in a good situation, is, the View and Prospect of a fine Country. . . . What Advantage would it be, to plant a Garden in a Place that is buried, and has no kind of Prospect? Such a Situation would be very disagreeable and unwholesome. . . . For my own part I esteem nothing more diverting and agreeable in a Garden, than a fine View, and a Prospect of a noble Country. The pleasures of seeing, from the End of a Walk, or off a Terrass, for four or five Leagues round, a vast Number of Villages, Woods, Hills, and Meadows, with a thousand other Varieties which make a beautiful Landscape, exceeds all that I can possibly say of it; a sight of these Things being the only Means to form a just Idea of their Beauty.'

Perhaps a view of this kind is not for us all. But we do have our compensations—enormous ones. Think today of the wide variety of cultivars we have (improved cultivars mostly) and of plants, compared even with Gertrude Jekyll's day. And think also that compared with her day, the Romans had only the rose, poppy, violet, iris and jasmine.

I have earlier on advised you to join the Royal Horticultural Society and in my last Chapter I do so again. There is the annual Show at Chelsea, the beautiful gardens at Wisley and the monthly editions of *The Journal of The Royal Horticultural Society*. *The Journal* in a year contains enough gardening wisdom to last a lifetime. And whilst referring to authoritative journals, there are the Ministry of Agriculture bulletins—you name your subject, there is bound to be a bulletin on it. Weekly too, there are those admirable journals *Popular Gardening* and *Amateur Gardening*.

There is very little other advice I can give, except perhaps to renew yourself each spring as the garden does. To realise that the gardener himself is part of a design, and that you are using, as a gardener, beautiful living things, which you do not own, but which are in your safe keeping for a time. You must realise this and give a good account of your stewardship.

This all sounds very serious, does it not? I'm sure one is not meant to be too serious in the garden. Have fun. The film director Billy Wilder once said 'Unless treated with humour, wit, and gaiety, even sex is unbelievably dull.' So it is with gardening.

Index of Plants and Trees for Cultivation

Note: Where more than one species is mentioned in the text this is indicated in the index by the abbreviation *sp.* similarly *var.* stands for variety or varieties.

186

General and Bibliographical Index